Beginning to Teach:
Primary Teaching Explained

Beginning to Teach:
Primary Teaching Explained

Clare Marlow

David Fulton Publishers
London

Published in association with the Roehampton Institute

David Fulton Publishers Ltd
2 Barbon Close, London WC1N 3JX

First published in Great Britain by
David Fulton Publishers 1994

Note: The right of the author to be identified as the author of this work has been
asserted by her in accordance with the Copyright, Designs and Patents Act 1988.

Copyright © Clare Marlow

British Library Cataloguing in Publication Data

A catalogue record for this book is available from the British Library

ISBN 1-85346-259-4

Typeset by RP Typesetters Ltd., Unit 13, 21 Wren Street, London WC1X 0HF.

Printed in Great Britain by BPCC Journals Ltd., Exeter.

Contents

The Roehampton Teaching Studies Series

This new series of books is aimed primarily at student and practising teachers. It covers key issues in current educational debate relating to age phases, school management, the curriculum and teaching methods. Each volume examines the topic critically, bringing out the practical implications for teachers and school organisation.

Authors – not necessarily based at Roehampton – are commissioned by an Editorial Board at The Roehampton Institute, one of the United Kingdom's leading centres of educational research as well as undergraduate and postgraduate training.

The General Editor of the series is Dr Jim Docking, formerly Chairman of the Institute's School of Education.

A selection of recent and forthcoming titles appears on the back cover of this book.

Introduction

This is a book for students at the beginning of their teacher-training for the primary years. With so much current debate about the state of education, it is an act of bravery to consider entering the profession at all. Luckily there will always be people who consider that they would find a happy and fulfilled professional life in the primary sector. Undoubtedly there are times in any teacher's work when she feels that she is pushing a pea uphill with her nose. But there are many other times when there is great joy and a feeling of satisfaction. It is a demanding job, and it asks for stamina and clear vision. This book will help you begin to make your own vision.

It may well be that the new format of teacher-training allows very little time for thinking about the principles that underlie all good teaching. As students you may well find yourselves going into classrooms with only a short time to prepare for teaching. It would be a pity if uncertainty led you to teach in a way that was not really how you wanted, but rather born of desperation. This book will guide you through some of your early anxieties about the content and style of your teaching, and help you make your own classrooms exciting places in which to learn.

Historical background

First, it is important that the current state of education is set in its historic framework, for only then will some of the debates that are raging be understood. It was 25 years ago, in 1967, that Lady Plowden and her committee identified a trend in teaching that they emphasised and advocated in the report they prepared for the government (The Plowden Report 1967). The trend became labelled 'child-centred education'. If only the journalists had thought of another phrase a lot of controversy would have been avoided. For a child-centred classroom, in the minds of people who never went into classrooms, conjured up an image of rampage and disorder. Even observers who did go into schools often failed to analyse what they were looking at and reported that 'all they do is play'.

The child-centred approach focussed on experiential learning, using Piaget's theories of child development as support. The child who was actively experimenting with apparatus or materials was assumed to be learning in a 'better' way than the child working from a textbook. Architects were inspired by this idea of self-generating workshop activities, and offered local authorities open-plan school buildings with bays, quiet areas and wet areas, to be used by groups rather than classes.

The late sixties and early seventies were times of great change. Teachers could see that the benefits of involving children in actively making decisions about their work were enormous. Group work became the norm, and textbooks were cut up throughout the land to make 'work cards'. Much more exciting art, music and drama began to appear from primary schools. Yet there were still misgivings, and they were not unfounded. Piaget's theories of child development, as they were often interpreted, were seen to be rather extreme in their insistence that the child had to 'discover' everything rather than be taught it in a more traditional way. Time was wasted in many classrooms as teachers held back from giving children ready-made answers, and waited for the discoveries to be made. Furthermore, instead of learning through separate subject areas, the children were introduced to historical, geographical and scientific concepts and facts through topic work. This could provide greater motivation, because the topics chosen were of interest to primary-age children, but the same topics could also include or leave out whatever the teacher decided. Thus, working across the subject areas, which was held by most teachers to be an appropriate way of teaching young children, often tended to give only a sketchy knowledge of each subject. This would not have been terribly important if the children had learned skills and concepts that would stand them in good stead for the rest of their lives. Unfortunately some teachers using the topic approach were accused of failing to provide this basic learning as well.

The Plowden phrase 'at the heart of the education process lies the child' was assumed by some people to mean that no curricular or organisational decisions could be made without consulting the child first. Some commentators saw the emphasis on the individual child as destroying all previously accepted educational theory.

> The main thrust of the argument outlined here is this, that to start from the standpoint of individual difference is to start from the wrong position. To develop effective pedagogic means involves starting from the opposite standpoint, from what the children have in common as members of the human species; to establish the general principles of teaching in the light of these, to determine what modifications of practice are necessary to meet specific needs.
> (Simon 1981)

From the moment schools began to become brighter, friendlier and more exciting places, some sections of public opinion seem to have been against their aims. Some of the opposition is understandable, for the reasons already given, but the attraction of the new-style schools could not be denied. It is almost as if there were a race memory in this country that expects schools to be like Bash Street School in *The Beano*. Any classroom that does not have a teacher standing at the front is labelled as 'progressive'. This is about as meaningless as labelling the Ford Fiesta a 'progressive' car because it is not like the Model T. Too often the term 'progressive' is applied disparagingly to a system that has been researched and modified for the last quarter of a century.

But what are the links between teaching style and learning? Researchers moved into the classroom and put the interaction of teacher and class under the microscope. Things were not always as they appeared:

> Bealing (1972) showed that while there had been a large-scale move towards the individualisation of the learning, there appeared to be little enthusiasm for group work of the kind recommended by the Plowden committee. Desks were pushed together to form tables around which typically sat five or six pupils, but these pupils worked on their own tasks individually.
> (Galton 1987)

Research carried out by the University of Leicester from 1975, and given the title ORACLE (Observational Research and Classroom Learning Evaluation) showed time and again that the styles of the teachers could vary enormously and still be included under the same 'progressive' banner. Sometimes teachers were giving the children a clear routine to work to; others were allowing the children to choose their activities; and yet others were frequently changing from one style of teaching to another. One important conclusion of this research showed that informal work in a classroom carries a risk of 'high ambiguity' for the children. Insecure children found ways of minimising the risk of 'getting it wrong' by undertaking simple undemanding tasks that would take up a lot of time. Teachers who want children to work independently must first spend time giving them the confidence and the knowledge they will need.

The National Curriculum

The National Curriculum for Primary Schools continues the tradition of informality which is now firmly in place in our schools. It puts an emphasis on active learning through genuine collaboration. However, to meet the kind of criticism which sees informality as an abandonment of responsibility, teachers are encouraged to be more aware of the coherence, progression, differentiation and above all the objectives behind every task. (All these terms will be discussed later in the book.)

Probably the greatest change that the National Curriculum has brought to the primary school is the requirement that all children be tested at the end of every Key Stage in order to assess the level each child has reached, and so help the teacher pin-point the teaching needed as he or she enters the next Stage. Yet even here, where greater accountability is being placed on schools, the tests are planned to take place as part of the school activities, and within normal teaching time. There was no suggestion made that an 'Eleven Plus' type test should be given.

None of these emphases suggest a return to a predominantly directive style of class teaching, although the teacher may want to work with the whole class together at certain times of the day. In order to reinforce and check learning at every stage, the National Curriculum places great importance on oracy, that underlying skill which not only shows the developing thinking of the child, but also helps the thinking to develop. Once a teacher has established a classroom ethos of articulate, non-judgemental discussion, then pathways are open between teacher and learner that have been closed for too long.

The Alexander Report on primary schools 1992

The government commissioned report on primary schools (Alexander et al 1992) tried once and for all to get behind the rhetorical debate between 'progressivism' and 'formality'. In it, the authors explain that there are many factors that affect a school's performance, and mediocrity of teaching is only one of them, but an important one, and one that should be addressed by the profession. They point to a lack of professional skills in some teachers, who rely on merely questioning and praising. Teachers should be able to analyse their teaching, they argue, and choose between a wide range of styles and tactics to get the best from their classes. These skills include planning, assessing, instructing, providing feedback, and using the methods of individual, group or classwork as best suits the activities. The report calls this 'fitness for purpose'. It will not be enough to pick up these classroom strategies and teaching techniques from the few teachers whose classes you work in; there must be the time and space for you to read books such as this, and make your own synthesis and style of teaching.

The Alexander Report also makes some points about the planning and implementation of topic work. It finds that too many topics are not well thought out, and only provide a poor introduction to the subjects they are intended to cover. The report calls for more specialist teaching at the top end of the primary school. It is very unlikely, however, that the appropriate staffing will be provided by local authorities (or governing bodies if the school controls its own budget). Specialist teaching is impractical in all but the largest primary or middle schools, so the class teacher has to continue to provide the specialist teaching herself over the whole range of the National Curriculum. This need not be such a daunting task as it sounds, as this book will show.

Reading

The debate about how to best teach reading has moved out of schools and into the public domain through the media. Everyone now feels that they are entitled to have a view on this subject, yet they are often rather poorly informed about what really goes on in schools. There has been a feeling in some quarters that children are not being taught to read, but rather given a selection of books and expected to get on with it. No wonder teachers have felt cross and misunderstood when they know how hard they work to help every child learn to read. In part, the fault may lie with schools who have not explained their methods sufficiently to parents.

Her Majesty's Inspectorate (HMI) produced a report for the government in the autumn of 1990, *The Teaching and Learning of Reading in Primary Schools,* based on a survey of 120 schools (HMI 1990). In contrast to the popular view they found that only 1 in 10 teachers did not teach phonics (the sounds that letters and groups of letters make) in some form or other, and they were mostly the teachers of older children who already possessed the skills. They go on to say:

> There was a clear link between higher standards and systematic phonic teaching. Phonic skills invariably formed part of the repertoire of those children who showed early success in reading. However, while the value of teaching these skills was rarely disputed, how and how often to teach phonics were more controversial issues. Some schools adopted popular published schemes for teaching phonic skills; others advocated a phonic approach as the teacher judged appropriate for individual children; some taught phonic skills incidentally or as an adjunct to an existing reading scheme which was not necessarily designed to promote such skills.
> (para. 31)

The Ofsted report of 1993 noted that teachers use a range of methods when teaching reading, but in the less successful classes 'they function more as an ad hoc mixture' (Ofsted, 1993). In the later chapter on reading and writing support, there will be suggestions to help you become one of the teachers who include planned and effective phonic teaching which gives children such a valuable skill in their early reading and writing.

'Real books'

The Press has also had much to say on the 'real books' issue. The term 'real books' has become the way in which books that are not part of a reading scheme are described. Teachers have felt that children should have access to the whole published collection of picture and story-books, rather than keep to the small set of graded readers, often written by the same author and with no great literary merit. This has led uninformed opinion to state that children's reading is not guided or taught in a logical progression. Again, the 1990 HMI report finds that this just is not true, and that only 5 per cent of teachers consider their approach as a 'real book' method, and that 95 per cent of schools are using graded readers though these are supplemented by other fiction and non-fiction (para. 29). The more varied provision of books of all kinds, and especially those of true quality, must be an incentive for any emergent reader.

Slower readers

It is ironic that at a time when there is a feeling that 'informality' may have been a screen for inadequate teaching methods, there is also a government initiative which advocates the ultimate in 'child-centred' approaches to help counter reading difficulties. Professor Marie Clay from New Zealand, who devised the Reading Recovery programme, has long been an advocate of studying the emergent reading and writing of individual children in order to be able to target teaching to match precisely their cognitive needs (Clay 1972 and 1979). She believes in using a broad range of techniques and is impatient with the way critics have polarised reading methods in the debate. It is Marie Clay's multi-method approach, targeted to individual needs that has been used by many local authorities for giving remedial help to slow readers, and it is these methods that are now receiving commendation from the government. It seems logical to believe that what is good for children who find reading hard to grasp must be equally good for children in general. Marie Clay's books do not provide a 'quick fit' solution to the teaching of reading, but they alert teachers to the importance of looking at the developmental stages of all children.

School and society

The debate about the effectiveness of our state education goes on and on. Some parents are more involved with their children's schools than ever before, and willingly give up hours of time to help in the classroom or accompany outings. At the same time, more parents than ever are choosing to send their children to private schools. What has made them take such a decision? Is it real knowledge of state schools or merely unfounded rumour? And what is it that makes private schools so appealing?

In staffrooms too there is a paradoxical situation. With the power to control their own budgets, schools are finding that they have less rather than more freedom. Money may not stretch to providing supply cover for teachers to go on professional courses. And services that used to be available from the local authority, such as school meals, speech therapy, special needs help, swimming lessons, music lessons, now have to be 'bought in', or may not exist at all. Head teachers may find themselves pressurised by governors to appoint a newly-qualified teacher rather than one with more experience because he or she will be cheaper.

The introduction and dissemination of the National Curriculum was very much a 'top down' exercise, and caused a great deal of confusion and anxiety among teachers. Now, after four years, there is a general feeling that teaching objectives have been clarified by its implementation, although the whole area of testing still remains an unresolved issue. Teachers feel that the tests have rarely told them anything they did not already know about the children's attainments. The publicising of school results in a league table caused great ill feeling in the profession too. Grammar schools in middle-class areas, which expected to do extremely well in academic exams, were compared with schools for slow-learners, where none of the children should even have been put in for exams. Teachers were unanimous in their opposition to such inappropriate competition: they could clearly see that children's best interests would not be served by such a system. Already there had been a great increase in the suspension of unruly children from secondary schools. If schools were to be judged solely by their academic results, then why should they bother with disciplining and caring for recalcitrant children who would not contribute to the exam successes at the end of their school life? The logical outcome of this would have been that difficult children ended up in 'sink' schools where resources were poor and little effort was made to achieve high standards in anything. The government withdrew the league tables after the first year.

Luckily, teachers always side with the children in any debate. It is the empathy which teachers feel to young people that has drawn them into the profession, and they will fight incessantly to maintain the best for them. We are fortunate in this country that we have a system of primary education that is admired throughout the world. Any interference from governments which puts the system at risk will be opposed by parents, teachers and governors alike. The best weapon against inappropriate changes is knowledge of the best practice that already exists.

Teachers have to learn to publicise themselves and their schools, and you as students can help too. We must all be ready to answer charges that schools do not teach children to read, to add up, to spell. We must point to the influences of society. In a television and video-game age the skill of literacy is devalued. In an age of materialism the values of tolerance and sharing are not much in evidence. In an age of competition the achievements of the less able are not rewarded. In such a society it is amazing what schools manage to do. They provide an environment of loving acceptance of difference, of celebration of small achievements, and of co-operative living which is a precious oasis in our society today. Students should look forward to becoming part of this wonderful world.

CHAPTER 1

The Successful Learner

What was the last thing you learned? How to drive, or how to use a word-processor? Or did you puzzle over some conflict reported on the news? And how successful were you?

Thinking of these experiences brings back the confused feelings we had when we were in the middle of the learning process. At first the subject seemed incomprehensible, and we felt uncertain whether we would ever get the hang of it. But, luckily for some of us, help was at hand, and we recount our relief: 'My daughter uses a word-processor at work so she helped me', we say, or, 'I had a very patient driving instructure', or, 'There was a good article with a map in the Sunday paper so I cut it out to keep.'

The parallels with children learning are clear. Learners of every age need teachers and good teaching aids to smooth the path that leads to new knowledge and skills. Not for nothing do we talk of 'an uphill struggle'. The journey is a hard one. The human brain is excellent at sorting out and classifying once it has enough data to work on. But in the early stages of learning any new thing, we lack the data or the experience to allow our brains to get to work. 'All those dials, knobs and sticks for my hands and three pedals for two feet,' thinks the learner driver. The driving instructure helps the learner to know which of the controls are of first importance, and which are only used occasionally, like the fog light switch, for example. Suddenly, there doesn't seem quite so much to take in, as our brains begin to make a pattern of the information we are receiving through our eyes and ears and body.

We can also remember what we felt like during the good learning experiences. Often our happy memories contain one of two things. First, we may have been praised for understanding or 'getting it right'. Secondly, we may have found that we were able to retell or explain our understanding to someone else. 'You have to copy your work on to a disc if you don't want to lose it. I'll show you what to do,' we say confidently to another struggling word-processor learner. We now know the procedure because we have made an effort to understand it, not because we learned it by rote. And we were learning not for a trivial reason, like getting points in a quiz, but because we felt inept and powerless without the knowledge. The subject or skill seemed important, our motivation was high. Sharing the knowledge with someone else is demonstrating that we now know what we are talking about.

Active learning

The successful child or adult learner is helped by a useful teacher smoothing the path. But the extremely useful teacher does another thing as well. At every step the teacher checks that the learner still understands and is actively involved rather than passively receiving information that is not making much sense. This is where active, 'hands on' experience is so useful as well as the chance to question and retell the new learning. To illustrate this, I have chosen the classroom scene of a teacher and a group of children watching a boiling kettle, and thinking about water becoming steam.

Example 1

T. Do you understand?
C. I think so.
T. Which bit don't you understand?
C. Well I don't really know which bit.
T. Shall I explain again?
C. (reluctantly) Yes please.

The teacher has the complete knowledge, the child apparently has none, although this is unlikely to be the true state of affairs. The knowledge is being delivered in a package and is useless. The ch8ild hasn't got the ability to open the package and take out the bit he or she needs, so the teacher delivers the whole package again.

Example 2

T. Do you understand?
C. No.
T. Do you see what the kettle is doing?
C. Yes, and we've got a kettle at home like that.

The child is clothing the theoretical in a familiar form, as best suits his cognitive stage of development. The concept of water turning into steam may not be understood, but the wise teacher listens to the unsophisticated reply and is then able to structure the rest of the lesson around this child. Perhaps this particular piece of concept learning, that water turns into steam, may be better left until the child is older.

Example 3

C1. Look here comes the steam
C2. Yes and it's whooshing now. Look at the water bubbling.
C1. Where's the steam going? Nowhere.
C2. In the air, nowhere.
C1. The water's making steam.

The teacher in this example is silent. Without her interventions we can hear what is going on loud and clear. The children are actively observing and thinking, putting their thoughts into words and answering each other. They are making solutions that are not correct, but they are at least thinking. Now that the children have become actively involved with the problem, the teacher can intervene to smooth out some misconceptions; the water isn't making steam, it is becoming steam; steam can't go nowhere, it can be turned back to water under the right conditions, such as on the cold windows, which is a process known as condensation, and so on. This last example shows how the teacher can be of most use and yet it looked as if the teacher was taking no part in the lesson.

Successful learners work in an atmosphere that is suited to them. As teachers, you have to listen to their conversations. This will help you pin-point where they have reached in their learning journeys and match your teaching to them. Information needs to be given, not in unfriendly packages, but in useful quantities that match the children's needs. Classroom discourse, if fostered sympathetically, can provide the key

4

to learning in every area of the curriculum. This is not a case of teaching 'formally' or 'informally', but the only way to make sure our teaching does not fall on deaf ears and leave mere confusion.

The examples of the boiling water experiment show us how varied children's responses can be and how many misconceptions may remain uncovered unless the teacher is constantly on the alert. When we consider the enormous task of learning to read, then the problems multiply. To read fluently is to perform an almost miraculous trick, as this quotation illustrates:

> Every articulate reading moment entails a switch of perspective, and this constitutes an inseparable combination of differentiated perspectives, foreshortened memories, present modifications, and future expectations. Thus, in the time flow of the reading process, past and future continually converge in the present moment, and the synthesising operations of the wandering viewpoint enable the text to pass through the reader's mind as an ever expanding network of connections. This also adds the dimension of space to that of time, for the accumulation of views and combinations gives us the illusion of depth and breadth, so that we have the impression that we are actually present in a real world.
> (Wolfgang Iser 1978, p.116)

It seems incredible that when you introduce children to stories and poems on the classroom mat, and help them read their first little books, you are starting them on the path to the kind of almost supernatural ability that is described in the quotation above. The children give clues about their reading development from the errors they make when reading aloud. The vigilant teacher uses these clues as evidence and tries to make her teaching as helpful as possible. The skill of literacy is so complicated and internalised, that it needs the greatest of skill to teach it successfully.

Motivation

Thinking back to our own learning experiences, and how often we found them an uphill struggle, gives us more clues about the best way to teach. As adult learners, we usually know why we are learning something when it is part and parcel of our everyday life: we want to cook a recipe from a magazine for a Saturday treat; we want to speak Spanish on holiday; we want to know more about growing vegetables.

Can we replicate this focus of motivation in the classroom?

Because classroom learning involves topics which are not simple reflections of children's felt needs, there has to be a little 'stage management' in the motivation that teachers offer children. In reality, the children are working on tasks the teacher has chosen in order to increase their literacy or numeracy. Nevertheless, there can be plenty of enjoyment in the work if the stage is set in an exciting way. Here are some examples of what a teacher might say to a class at the beginning of a session:

1a. It would be nice to send Emma something while she is in hospital.
1b. We're all going to make get well cards for Emma.

2a. Cut this card for wheels and use the dowelling for axles.
2b. Model vehicles are more fun if the wheels go round.

3a. The red group are going to make a diagram of the food chain they have investigate.
3b. The red group need to think how to explain the food chain to the other groups.

In one mode the teacher is giving an instruction and in the other she is making a statement or suggestion, and it isn't hard to see which is which. The statements are of course disguised commands, and are a trick of teaching. The children are still being asked to do something, yet there is an atmosphere of choice and autonomy suggested by the wording of the statements which gives the learners great motivation. The style of the classroom used by such a teacher will leave more room for initiative. Because one teacher is in charge of 30 children, any egalitarianism has to be seriously modified. Children are invited to take some decisions but not all: this is not a free for all. They cannot choose to do something dangerous. Nor can they choose to do nothing. But with an interesting task, interestingly presented, they will be more motivated to try hard and achieve a good result.

Learners also need time to reflect and internalise what they have just received as new information. This can be done in a variety of ways, but there is often very little attention given to this process during teaching. Teachers move straight from giving new information to expecting the children to be able to produce work using this information. Some teachers ask children for written work as proof of their understanding.

Others plan for a session of oral work, where children explain to one another what they have just learned. This may strike you as very like the system at college, where you are asked either to write essays or deliver seminars on subjects within your syllabus. You know, from your own experience, that you only felt ready to write the essay or give the seminar after a great deal of preparation. This was the time you needed to internalise the information and arguments you had first been introduced to in the lectures you had attended. Children need this time in the same way. Many of the activites in the primary classroom are more valuable than they appear precisely because they provide this reflective time. So a group of children apparently arguing endlessly on how to make a windmill or a suspension bridge, are in fact clarifying their thoughts and making the theoretical a practical reality in their own minds.

Summary

In this chapter it has been suggested that successful learning in the classroom depends upon certain factors: the provision of useful learning aids; the feeling of success; the time to talk and ponder on new information; the careful intervention of a teacher who is in tune with the state of the learner; the sense of motivation; the chance to teach others about the newly acquired knowledge; the feeling that the learner has some control over the tasks.

CHAPTER 2

The Successful Teacher

Considering yourself

When we say 'I loved Chemistry at school', or 'I was very interested in art', what we are probably saying is 'My art/chemistry teacher made the subject exciting for me.' The love of the subject is what we carry with us for the rest of our lives, but it was often the teacher who put the interest there in the first place. How rewarding to inspire children in this way. It is the greatest delight of any teacher, and one of the greatest motivations to enter the profession.

There is no reason why any teacher cannot achieve this, with some children at least. First, you need to examine yourself, to reflect upon what your own enthusiasms are. For it is in these areas that you will be the most effective as a teacher. The subjects of your enthusiasms need not be 'school' subjects as such, but, if you acknowledge them, they can be used for the benefit of the children. For example, an enthusiast's knowledge of birds and the methods of bird-watching gives you a good ground in all areas of the natural sciences. Through your experience of delight in bird watching, and the awareness of how meticulous you have to be in this study, you can initiate the children into the study of anything else – worms, moths and even, through the use of films and books, African mammals or Antarctic wildlife. The basic scientific principles will be taught more effectively if you have had a grounding in some area of research.

Similarly, if you like to sew and embroider, you can approach any craft area with the same attention that you pay to your own hobby. For example, you know from experience that it is good practice to keep materials clean and separated from each other, and to store your unfinished work in a well-ordered way. By offering the children a serious, craft-like approach, you can, by example, indicate that the work is important, and that you expect high standards of effort and achievement.

Having considered your strengths and enthusiasms, you now have to think about your weaknesses. For many primary teachers, the opportunity to teach across the curriculum is one of the main attractions of the job. Detailed programmes outlined in the National Curriculum documents have shown many teachers that there is more to certain subjects than they were aware of. Indeed, a recent government report (Alexander et al 1992) has suggested that children need more specialist teaching at the top end of the primary school. Subject expertise is a difficult area to establish: some of the most knowledgeable people make the worst teachers, especially at primary level. Primary schools alleviate the problem by dividing the specialisms between the staff so there is a pool of specialist knowledge to draw upon during planning and teaching. There is a need, however, for every teacher to become 'good' at every subject they are teaching, and to make good the deficit in the subjects in which they feel weakest. It isn't enough to say, 'I'm hopeless at history', when there is a requirement to teach history.

For some teachers entering the profession, there is a lot of learning to be done in such areas as music or P.E., for example. Now that the National Curriculum is in place, the whole of it has to be given to each child by statutory right. This can only improve children's educational opportunities. However, there are times when every teacher longs not to have the responsibility of her least favourite area. This is where you would be well advised to look for good books or schemes of work that map out the subject in a clear way. If the scheme appeals to you, and is approved by the school you are working in, then it will take a load off your mind. Studying the National Curriculum, alone or in a staff group, will also help you to see the subject more clearly in terms of teaching objectives. In this respect, in the next chapter there is an exercise on the English programmes of study for you to work through. Once you are in your first job, there will be courses you can go on to give you extra help in certain areas.

Filling in the gaps of your own education is one of the bonuses of primary teaching. When you start to unravel the subject at a level suitable for children, you often find a great deal of pleasure in it. The reference and textbooks that are available in all children's libraries are such a delight to read, that you become envious of the children of the 1990s who have such good resources. For many adults, learning from these modern texts and videos becomes a real delight, and the old phobias and blanknesses disappear. Also, learning a subject with a view to teaching it is a great way to sort it out in your mind. There is no room for being hazy, so you learn efficiently. Remember, you are not learning a subject to get a Ph.D., but to be able to give children a serious and coherent grounding. The subject matter needs to be accurate and up to date, but it needn't be enormously extensive, and there is nothing wrong with saying 'I don't know' when children ask you things, provided you promise to find out or help the children to do so.

One of the most important parts of your teaching should be that you are giving the children appropriate tools for learning: how to use reference books to find information efficiently; how to tackle evidence in the geographical, historical or scientific fields, and what to do with this evidence; how to read texts critically. The methods of learning that you introduce to the children in the primary school could be the methods they use for the rest of their lives. The subject matter is not so important as the ways of learning about the subject, and the activities you plan should provide a coherent pathway.

Thinking like a teacher

When student teachers first prepare activities for a group of children to work on, they usually have plenty of good ideas and they usually get the level of learning about right. But they often forget that children do not behave intellectually like mini-adults. Children will only begin to show interest in a subject if their imagination is aroused, and this is often achieved by using narrative or story as the basis of the subject. For example, a study of the Antarctic might be approached as a geographical investigation into the landscape of snow and ice. Or it could be a study of the various types of penguins that live there. But for children, the story of Shackleton's exploration or Scott's ill-fated journey would give a basis for the other studies, and provide a dramatic and moving story as well. The archive material from Scott's expedition can easily be found in textbooks, and it carries with it the authentic flavour of misplaced courage that children can respond to. They will learn about penguins and icebergs as well, but have a much greater and longer-lasting picture of the severity of conditions on the Antarctic continent.

Narrative is central to the child's eye view of the world. Children make their first picture-books objects of the greatest importance, and they make-believe so easily when they play either together or alone. This evidence gives you an inkling as to how significant story is. Teachers who remember this always keep narrative as the core to all their teaching. They make time to bring stories and poetry to the children's attention every day. In this way the children will know what books can offer them and become readers with self-motivation rather than reluctant learners of reading principles. The choice of stories is important. Despite the wonderful selection that publishers offer, it is all too easy to give children stories that are predominantly Eurocentric, with white male central characters. There will be an exploration of some of the gender and race issues involved in the choice of literature in the chapter on reading and writing (chapter 6) as well as a discussion about the general choice of books at all stages.

Significance and quality

The successful teacher is someone who has not forgotten what it feels like to be a child, and yet is able to add adult perceptions to these memories. All primary teachers have a wonderful opportunity to create, in their own rooms, the environment they would like to learn in if they were children. As you remember your own childhood, how important certain toys and books were, and how important textures of furniture, smells of places, sounds of things, were to you, you can begin to create your classroom. Objects, pictures, the layout of the furniture, the place to sit and be together, are all under your control. The two necessities to remember here are quality and significance. Children will respond to high quality in their environment by behaving well and taking care of things. It is a pity, though, that teachers often have to endeavour to create a high quality environment in such poor quality buildings.

Significance is an over-used word in books about teaching. But just as the toys and objects from your childhood are invested with significance in your own mind, so you can prepare the environment of your classroom to have the same significance for the children who learn there. All that you bring into the room should be of good quality, and have intrinsic interest for the children. In Victorian schools there may have been only one picture and perhaps a map on the wall. Nowadays, there is so much for children to look at and listen to and play with, that it is almost *more* difficult to engage their interest. But a few principles may help you choose what to offer them. There will be a more detailed look at display in the chapter about topic work.

First, displays are arranged in classrooms for many reasons, but the main one is to aid learning. Learning is an active process, so the best displays contain an element of interaction. This means that children can perhaps take words from a display and reorder them, or move labels on a picture, or maybe put cards in order on a flow chart. All these things are very easy to organise with sticky pads on the back of cardboard. Children's artwork can be labelled, not just with the names, but with little comments or questions to the artist. 'Ask Katy about the people in this picture', is an invitation to the children to talk together, and shows that you take Katy's picture seriously. And the card doesn't take much longer to write than the usual 'Katy Smith'. Not all displays that you create need to be interactive in this way. Sometimes it is very pleasant to have a corner of the room arranged purely for aesthetic enjoyment.

Secondly, teachers should think about every piece of apparatus, every construction game, every work card they have in their classroom as part of their teaching. It is interesting to notice that other teachers' equipment never seems quite right when you come to use it. This is because the choice is such a personal one. The style of your work is mirrored by the things you use in your work, and teachers spend long hours making charts and work cards that suit their own needs and the perceived needs of their class. This seems like a waste of time, but is, in fact, part of the search for a style and ideology that begins when you first start working with children. An art advisor was humourously scathing when he visited the school I was working in. 'Why do you all try to make your room look like Debenhams?' he asked. But it isn't just a matter of window dressing to want to bring colour, design and quality to our work.

Thirdly, the way you teach and the materials you choose to teach with are linked in a more fundamental way. There must be an ideological base to your teaching, which you can justify if challenged, and which you reflect in your choice of teaching environment. A simple example might be the way in which you use your own handwriting around the room, on work cards and in the children's books. When you pay attention to the script you use, trying to make it a good model for the children to copy, you are signalling that presentation and pride in the finished product is important. Writing evenly and in the school's chosen style takes practice, but, as in the subject learning mentioned before, it can be very enjoyable. Buying good thick marker pens and making well-presented wall charts is satisfying work and students often surprise themselves with their newly discovered talent.

Another example will demonstrate the ideological basis behind every piece of work you introduce. Suppose the children are studying trees and you decide to make a display of objects made of wood. It will be easy to collect some wooden spoons, a bowl, some children's bricks, and so on. Thinking more deeply about the subject, though, you may decide that there are more interesting things you can do as well. In the past wood was used for things that are now made of plastic; and today plastic is sometimes disguised to look like wood. Your collection could now include some wooden toys to compare with plastic ones, old and modern clocks, wooden and plastic doorknobs, and perhaps some wood-grained plastic (Formica). Asking the children to speculate on why these changes have occurred through time will enlarge the learning about trees to include ideas about supply and demand, conservation of wood, and fashion.

A fourth and last point about the teaching environment is that it is the children's domain. During term-time they spend longer in their classroom than in their sitting-rooms at home. Although the room is densely populated, they manage to make themselves a space which becomes their own, possibly next to a special friend, and they often like to mark their space with pencil cases and other equipment. Decisions about the layout of the furniture and the placing of displays can be made by the teacher and the children together. In this way the children will have a positive attitude towards school and learning.

Teaching skills

Any exploration of how schools teach must first ask 'What are schools for?' The answer must be that they pass on the knowledge, skills and attitudes that society considers important. Teachers work together with their pupils and create

> a joint version of things encoded symbolically, in which shared understandings become established through the development of a common language and a common discursive element.
> (Edwards and Mercer 1989)

A good teacher wants to develop the skills needed to foster a rich and productive discourse in the classroom. The following list is only one way of exploring just what it is that good teachers do.

1. Presents problem clearly and makes task clear.
2. Creates ethos.
3. Good listener.
4. Sensitivity.
5. Protects minority views.
6. Provokes and asks for reasons to support views.
7. Asks open questions.
8. Avoids making statements.
9. Keeps discussion relevant to subject.
10. Encourages pooling of knowledge.
11. Provides information when asked.
12. Avoids stating own opinion.

(Trevor Kerry 1981)

Piaget's theories of learning have had a great influence on teaching in this country for the last 30 years. He saw the child as a little explorer, who had to discover every new concept for himself. During the last decade there has been a greater interest in the part that language plays in the development of cognition. The work of Vygotsky has become widely known. He was a Russian, who died in 1934 at the age of 37, and his work was not published or translated for many years because his ideas did not find favour with the Russian authorities. He saw human development as being a potential that can be awakened with interaction, and that language is the key to this interaction. He defined a 'zone of proximal development':

> The zone of proximal development defines those functions that have not yet matured but are in the process of maturation, functions that will mature tomorrow but are currently in an embryonic state. These functions could be termed the 'buds' or 'flowers' of development rather than the 'fruits' of development.
> (Vygotsky 1978)

Teaching which concentrates on this zone will be the most useful, because at this stage the child learns with help from the teacher. Closely connected with Vygotsky's theories is Bruner, who suggested that this help given to an apprentice learner be called 'scaffolding' (Bruner 1976). This support can help the learner achieve success and satisfaction, and gradually the scaffolding can be removed as the learning becomes firmly established. This is how children learn at home from their families. Perhaps teachers should try to behave more like parents and carers at home. This pattern of teaching has been called 'guided participation', or 'assisted performance', and typically consists of the following stages:

1. Providing a bridge between familiar skills or information and those needed to solve the new problem.

2. Arranging and structuring the problem.

3. Gradually transferring the responsibility for managing the problem-solving to the child.
(Rogoff B. and Gardner W. P. 1984)

Many researchers have looked at the interactions during a lesson and tried to find what it is specifically that makes a good teacher. It appears that academic aims are best met by a fairly 'formal' style of teaching, and that social and emotional goals are better met with 'informal' methods. Some characteristics of effective teaching have also been observed. They include:

momentum [freedom from slow-downs]
variety and challenge
smoothness [particularly at transition points]
with-it-ness [monitoring of all pupils]
overlappingness [dealing with several things at once]
(Kounin 1970)

Coping with social disadvantage

The primary teaching report of 1992, commissioned by Kenneth Clarke, the Education Secretary, contains the following statement: 'There has been a tendency to stereotype and to assume that social disadvantage leads inevitably to educational failure' (Alexander et al 1992). For many teachers, this criticism is obviously unfair and ungrounded. But there is some truth in the remark, and it is not difficult to see how the situation has arisen. When children come from backgrounds where nothing is certain and safe, either emotionally or financially, many teachers are aware of the huge gulf between the home and school environment. For children like this, security and happiness are the first requirement, ¬nd only then will they be able to be receptive to teaching. No wonder then that teachers have been less insistent that they achieve in areas of scholastic success, when they have so much to contend with merely adapting to a school routine and learning the rules of behaviour that are needed to operate in a group.

Some of the same considerations apply to children who come to school with little or no English. Luckily, the ability to learn a second language is at its height in the early years, and the normal socialising of the children while they work and play often teaches the child the new language in a remarkably short space of time. But when the job of learning to be literate in this new language is added to the initial spoken language learning, many teachers realise that literacy learning will have to be postponed for a few months at least. Here again, teachers are criticised for not applying more rigorous standards. Children with English as a second language did consistently worse in the reading and writing tests for seven-year-olds in 1991. The implications of this are quite frightening if a school's success is to be judged by these results.

For children with social disadvantage, and for those with little knowledge of spoken English, the teacher has to make many difficult decisions about what to expect of them. Outside their families, the class teacher is in a position to get to know the children better than anyone else, and only by making a professional judgement about their ability and readiness for learning will the teacher be able to help the children do their best. Whatever the background of the child, the teacher must constantly remind herself that each child is potentially a high achiever.

Recording achievement

The successful teacher has always had a clear idea in her head about the actual work and the potential of each child in her care. She has been able intuitively to offer the children the next appropriate step in the subject they are learning. This intuition is invaluable, but nowadays it is not enough on its own, for teachers have to provide evidence of their intentions, and proof that these have been carried out, for example by testing. Although the most publicised innovation of the National Curriculum, testing is only one stage in the process of planning with objectives in mind, teaching with the same objectives, and testing to see how far the objectives have been realised. The Standard Assessment Tasks (commonly referred to as SATS) at the end of every Key Stage, are only one form of test; there are many other, more

16

informal, means by which the teacher keeps a clear picture in her head about how much learning is taking place, rather than the amount of teaching that has been done, which can be very different.

Students should not fear this new emphasis on accountability. To be properly prepared with clear objectives for your teaching is to have a weight taken off your mind when it comes to the day-to-day running of the class. Building in to your programmes of work the opportunity to test the newly learned material is also helpful, as it gives you valuable clues for planning the next stage of your teaching.

Summary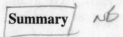

In this chapter some of the factors that make a successful teacher have been discussed. They include: having enthusiasm for the subject; knowing the subject well enough to introduce the study of it; understanding how children think (the importance of narrative); planning a teaching environment which will encourage learning; aiming for quality in all displays and materials used for teaching; recognising that each child is potentially a high achiever; having a repertoire of teaching skills.

CHAPTER 3

The Differentiated Day

This chapter will be about how to teach in a varied, interesting way. It will consider the importance of routine, and the equal importance of innovation in the school timetable. It will also consider ways of organising the children so that you make the best use of your time and expertise.

For teaching in primary schools to be effective today, three broad kinds of educational need must be borne in mind:

1. The need to deliver the National Curriculum.
2. The need to provide variety in teaching style and curriculum organisation.
3. The need to group children optimally for effective learning.

Taken together, these considerations require that the school offers children a 'differentiated' day, that is one in which learning is organised in a way that best suits the subject and offers the children the most interesting and active role. We shall now examine some teaching implications of each of the above needs.

The National Curriculum

At the heart of teaching today lies the National Curriculum, which lays out a body of knowledge and skills to be acquired at the various stages. Ostensibly, it is not concerned with the 'how' of the curriculum; this is left to the discretion of schools, who should produce their own policy documents. However, the Programmes of Study give suggestions about strategies and organisation. If these are adopted, they provide a wide range of activities which will ensure that the children experience a varied collection of things to do. There has been a tendency, in the early years of the National Curriculum, for teachers to consider only the Attainment Targets, and forget that the process of learning is as important as the product of that learning. Referring to the Programmes of Study is a way of reminding ourselves just how wide the range of activities has to be to ensure that children are getting all the experiences they need to fulfil the demands of the Curriculum. For example, the ability to maintain a point of view in a discussion group (English AT1, Talking and Listening, Level 4c) will not be practised if the class teacher never organises the children into discussion groups. The Programmes of Study suggest various ways in which these groups could operate.

On the following two pages, there is an activity which serves as an introductory look at the Programmes of Study for English in Key Stages 1 and 2. In the speech bubbles there are 26 statements or questions from teachers or children that you might hear in a primary classroom. You are asked to identify which area of study they are part of, by writing the letter or number of the remark against the points taken from the Programmes of Study which are listed on the left-hand side of each page. By doing this you will realise that much of what is recommended is covered by a well-chosen range of activities in a well-organised class. Some of the remarks in the speech bubbles could be put into several categories. You might like to do this activity with someone else, and debate your reasons for choosing the categories from the Programmes of Study.

Variety in teaching style and curriculum organisation

There are many classrooms which are organised on the 'integrated day' principle. Many of these are Key Stage 1 (infant) classes, but the system is also used with the Key Stage 2 (junior) age range. The idea is that children move around in groups, from one activity to another during the day, and cover a variety of tasks by the time they go home. This style of organisation has much to recommend it, especially as it allows the teacher to find tasks that children can do on their own, leaving herself time to spend with other groups that need her input and support.

The big disadvantage of this system is that days tend to be the same from start to finish, and each day much like another. This chapter has the title 'The Differentiated Day' because many teachers think it is better to find ways of marking different sessions for the children to give them more of a focus and motivation for their work. The integrated

National Curriculum for English Key Stages 1 & 2

What teachers should aim for (from Programmes of Study)

A

- continuity
- progression
- differentiation (between children)
- coherence (between language components)
- content
- reporting achievements
- breadth (across language curriculum)
- cross-curricular themes
- school policies
- LEA policies
- raising standards

Teachers' comments

B

Match a statement from B with an objective from A

Studying the stream for 3 weeks in the spring term is how we cover science, maths and language.

The blue group are putting the place names from our trip in alphabetical order.

The topics are planned for the whole school and I choose mini-topics myself.

Don't forget to take notes while you watch the video. They will help you with your drama.

Mrs Khan is going to help the yellow group with their spelling.

You must use evidence to back up your statement that the stream is polluted.

The county RE policy has a lot of good ideas for drama.

Every class has a 10 minute handwriting lesson three times a week.

They don't write every day but they talk about word formations. There will be more emphasis on writing next term.

Yes, but why didn't you like the book? Can you think of 2 reasons?

You're going to work in the same way as you did when we made the space travel book.

Mr & Mrs Harris, please look at the book Alison wrote for the infants in class 2.

National Curriculum for English Key Stages 1 & 2

Children's comments on their work

Match a statement from B with an objective from A

A — What children should be doing (from Programmes of Study)	B

A — What children should be doing (from Programmes of Study)

- sharing books
- enjoying language
- responding to story
- learning through language
- linking reading, writing, listening, talking
- achieving success in writing
- drawing on cultural identity
- working with others
- asking questions
- initiating ideas
- sustaining ideas
- evaluating own work

B

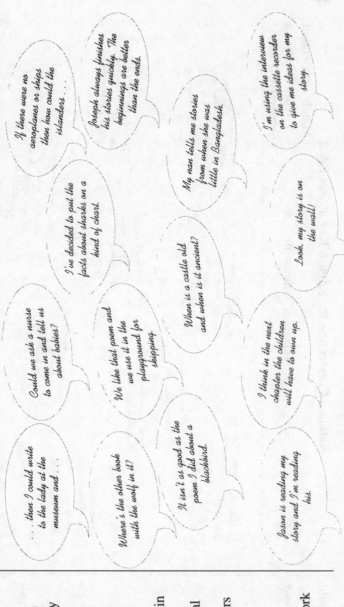

If there were no aeroplanes or ships then how could the islanders . . .

Joseph always finishes his stories quickly. The beginnings are better than the ends.

My nan tells me stories from when she was little in Bangladesh.

I'm using the interview on the cassette recorder to give me ideas for my story.

I've decided to put the facts about sharks on a kind of chart.

When is a castle old and when is it ancient?

Look, my story is on the wall!

Could we ask a nurse to come in and tell us about babies?

We like that poem and we use it in the playground for skipping.

I think in the next chapter the children will have to own up.

. . . then I could write to the lady at the museum and . . .

Where's the other book with the wolf in it?

It isn't as good as the poem I did about a blackbird.

Jason is reading my story and I'm reading his.

system is not out of favour, but there is a place for considering how teachers can make the best use of the repertoire of teaching skills, so that each part of the day is organised in a distinctive way and with a greater sense of purpose. When you visit classes identify how the teacher is changing her teaching style at different times of the day and why she is doing this. If the style remains the same, consider how the children respond. If they show signs of boredom or disruption try to identify the causes. If the children are happy and busy, then again you can identify what it is that the teacher is doing to keep up their motivation.

Teachers across the country are finding that the National Curriculum has demanded that they find time for far more history, geography, science, technology, music, drama and art. This has squeezed the time that is spent specifically on literacy and numeracy which, in these days of accountability, has worried many teachers. The National Curriculum tried to meet this concern by identifying some cross-curricular skills that can be practised while studying a variety of subjects. These are communication skills, numeracy, study skills, problem-solving, personal and social skills, and information technology. When thinking about a differentiated day, it is as well to remember that time is short, and that every effort should be made to make links across the curriculum.

In later chapters there will be detailed discussions about the processes of talking, reading and writing, with plenty of examples of activities. For the moment, the organisation of a differentiated day will be explored without such detail.

There are two initial principles which effective teachers try to observe. The first is to achieve a balance between practice or consolidation work, and introducing new ideas. Teachers need to consider this balance: too much routine and the children will become bored little robots; too much exciting novelty and they will become bewildered or over-excited nuisances who constantly need restraining.

The balance between novelty and routine is one of the hardest things for the student teacher to judge. This is primarily because the student comes into a class which already has its routine set by the class teacher. If the student feels that more novelty is called for, she needs also to bear in mind that changing the balance of the routine is very difficult in five or six weeks. At the same time, the children are aware that the student is not their permanent teacher, and look to her to provide them with a break in their routine. Students may respond to this feeling by organising plenty of exciting activities, as well as outings and visitors, so much so that the children may forget there ever was a routine, and begin to be a bit boisterous. At this point, students can feel a bit despondent, and feel they are 'losing control'. This is an unfair judgement, for the children are in reality paying the student a compliment by their enthusiasm. It is, therefore, often best for the student to resist making radical changes, but instead take on the organisation that is already in place, though modifying it a little to make room for new ideas. A teaching practice in a room that is organised by someone else will never provide the ideal environment in which to try out the full range of newly-acquired teaching skills, and the children will seldom respond to the student as they would to a class teacher. Only when the student has become an appointed member of staff will there be the real chance to fix routines as she wants them, and to balance these with new and stimulating experiences in a way she judges to be appropriate.

The second initial principle involves providing a structure which encourages a sense of purposefulness in the classroom. One of the most important rules to remember is that we listen best when we have to act on what we are listening to in the near future. This human trait is a good one on which to plan your classroom activities. Children are usually gathered together at the beginning of the morning and afternoon sessions. Here they answer the register and are told about their tasks for the next hour or so. This is a good idea, but the introductory session often goes on too long, with individual children holding forth about their birthdays and outings. Quite properly, the teacher likes to feel that this is enhancing the family side of classroom life, as well as giving children good practice in speaking to the others, and so it is. But the main points of instruction are often lost, and the children can become unfocussed and uncertain when they finally approach their work.

It seems essential to good teaching to be clear what we are doing at all times. The sharing of news is a time for being together in a family way. The time when you give information about the work you want groups or individuals to do is a time for listening carefully with a view to taking action immediately afterwards. The teacher, therefore, needs to signal clearly to the children that 'sharing time' is over, and that now 'listening carefully time' is beginning. Children waste a lot of time if they are left in a group with inadequate preparation or understanding of the task in hand. Some teachers have been rather diffident about giving instruction, feeling it has overtones of Victorian didactic teaching. But concepts and ideas do need to be explained, and information needs to be given if the principle of purposefulness is to characterise your classroom. Equally, the enthusiastic teacher who knows how to use objects, books, videos, pictures, maps and broadcasts will have a receptive audience of motivated pupils.

Grouping children optimally for effective learning

Another important way in which a day can be 'differentiated' is by grouping children differently according to the needs of the task in which they are engaged. The effective teacher organises her classroom so that at varying times the children are working as a class, in groups, in pairs or individually. Recent government reports on curriculum organisation and classroom practice in primary schools education (Alexander et al 1992, Ofsted 1993), stress that the choice between individual, group or whole-class teaching should be made, not on the basis of a dogma, but from a professional analysis of the task and the learners. There should be a 'fitness for purpose' in every activity in the classroom.

Whole-class learning

The normal timetable of a primary school has certain fixed points in the day when whole-class activities have to take place. These are often the times when the class has the use of the hall for P.E. or the grass outside for games, or the music room for singing or playing instruments. To give the day some shape, however, the teacher could also plan other times for class instruction or class activities. Many teachers have found that writing is best done when the room is quiet, and so they organise writing sessions as a whole-class activity. At these times, everyone in the class is engaged in individual writing tasks, without the distraction of other kinds of activity in the room. The atmosphere becomes one of creative endeavour, which would not be possible if some children were painting or making a noise with a model crane they were testing.

Class teaching best takes place when the teacher considers it appropriate for herself to be the most important resource for knowledge in the classroom. The subject matter that will underline part of a topic, for instance, can be delivered to the class in an exciting way, by planning a whole-class session. The discussion that arises from this lesson might then indicate that the class should pursue the next step in groups, but the initial input is most efficiently delivered to the class as a whole. These sessions of whole-class learning have been rather a rarity in the integrated day type of class organisation, but they are valuable in that resources can be shown and the shape of the topic can be explained. Children like to know where they are going in their learning.

Whole-class learning is one of the most efficient ways of giving the children information, or explaining concepts and ideas. The drawbacks are that some children will not fully understand what is said to the group because they need a more personal form of instruction. Other children will quickly grasp the points being made, and need not spend so long listening to the explanation. This is not significant if the teacher differentiates between the children during other sessions of work. Some children will need support by further explanations and discussions. Others may need to be asked to do more stretching things with the information they have received.

Group learning

It has already been mentioned in chapter 1 that, despite the teacher's intentions, children working around a table are often working alone because there is little collaboration between the members of the 'group'. This can be solved by showing the children that you take talk, (as distinct from chatter) seriously, and you expect them to offer to help each other. This change of ethos may take longer than a teaching practice to establish. The feeling of loneliness when working in a 'group' is one you may remember from your own schooldays, and it is not a constructive feeling that encourages effort. The children will work better if they feel that there are plenty of chances for sharing and checking their work. An example of group endeavour might be the creation of a guidebook about the school. The group could make decisions about who interviews the caretaker, who asks the secretary for information, who writes, who draws, who plans the layout. The children know each others' strengths and weaknesses, and should be encouraged to offer and receive help. They may have to be taught how to be constructively critical in their comments, so that they say 'This bit isn't very clear', rather than 'This bit is rubbish.' Building in discussion and consensus at every stage of producing written work is the ideal way both to cover as many requirements of the National Curriculum for English as possible, and provide a balance of individual, pair, group and class sessions.

With practice, groups can become expert at working collaboratively. For example, groups could be asked to 'brainstorm' to collect words that could be used for a poem about darkness. The poem could then be written jointly by using the chosen words in phrases and sentences. In a science lesson, groups could be asked to work out a way of testing how much a litre of water weighs. And in a history lesson, groups might be asked to look at illustrations of farm implements and decide which ones were in use a hundred years ago before drawing them for a picture of a Victorian farm. Younger children could work in groups to draw round their feet, cut them out and arrange them in order on a large piece of paper. In all these examples it will be the debates and decision-making that provide the valuable thinking and learning.

Individual learning

Every class teacher knows the individuals in her class almost as well as their parents do. The time that is spent with each child is unavoidably limited, so, for this reason alone, it must be time well spent. Giving a child some undivided attention will help his or her motivation better than anything else. By listening carefully to children's responses, a teacher can understand how they think, and can then choose the best way of explaining new ideas. This differentiation between children is very important because they all learn in their own way. Unfortunately, individual learning is the least efficient method of classroom organisation, at least as far as time is concerned. Many teachers realise that the school session time is not long enough to allow for individual chats. That is why you find teachers giving up their lunch-breaks and playtimes to concentrate on one or two children. Engaging in a one-to-one conversation with pupils is essential if teachers are to get to the root of children's learning problems and plan work to match their attainment levels. Fortunately, without using your coffee time, there are plenty of ways of organising time for individual teaching and assessment. For example, in infant classrooms there is less of a distinction between work and play. A group of children can be quite usefully engaged in building with construction toys, or playing with

26

sand or water. This gives the teacher a chance to concentrate on individuals. As children get older they become more independent in their work, and again, groups can be left with minimal supervision while some individual teaching is going on.

Other aspects of the differentiated day

Coherence and progression

The National Curriculum documentation uses these two terms when it urges teachers to plan their objectives with rigour. By 'coherence' it means that the work children do should match their cognitive development. If some aspects of the work are too easy and some too hard then children will not move smoothly forward in their learning because they will be bored or frustrated. By 'progression' it means that the tasks should follow each other in a way that matches the logical development of the subject. For example, what would be the logical development of learning about maps? Obviously the youngest children at school could be introduced to bird's-eye views of table-tops with objects on them. The next stage might be the drawing of the school, again 'as if a bird was looking down'. Ideas about symbols and scale will follow as the child gets older. Finally, the conventions of map-makers are explained, and the children become efficient users of maps and atlases for the rest of their lives. The National Curriculum was implemented to ensure that this kind of step-by-step progression is followed by every school and for every subject.

Using the facilities

A classroom is really a collection of learning contexts. One of the strengths of the 'informal' style of teaching has been the way that classrooms have been arranged to help children learn. You will typically find reading corners, writing corners, listening corners, craft tables, imaginative home corners, all fitted into rooms that were originally basic and boring. Having paid attention to the furniture and apparatus needed for these areas, the teacher has to consider her objectives for each child in using the facilities. This is where thinking has sometimes been rather unfocussed and woolly.

There are limits to the amount a five-year-old child can discover when left alone with bottles and funnels at a water tank. Here it would be appropriate to suggest, perhaps, things for the children to attempt, such as filling large bottles with water from smaller cups. This will introduce them to the principles of capacity which they will return to more formally at a later stage. Another example could be given from the home corner, where much imaginative play goes on. The wise teacher can use this play as the raw material for some more formal drama, or maybe for written work. For example, a home corner could become a doctor's waiting-room and surgery. The children can 'play' at writing appointments in a book and writing prescriptions. Older children, say seven-year-olds, could use the home corner for a nursery, where they pretend to feed and look after babies. The teacher could then make them aware of the parallels of baby-care in the animal world, and the children could then research into how various animals look after their young. As the subject matter will be close to the children's emotional hearts, it will be charged with significance.

It would be a pity not to use this significance as much as possible. The activities of a classroom should not be allowed to take place in separate vacuums, but be drawn together for all to learn from, and used as part of the literacy, numeracy and scientific processes as much as possible. Many activities which are given to the children as part of a topic are under-used in terms of learning possibilities, and this is often because the class remains fragmented about the room for the majority of the day.

Schools often have facilities for learning that have been forgotten or are just ignored. The grounds of a school can provide plenty of practical work in science, maths and geography, and children can get out into the neighbourhood to survey traffic or list shops, for example. Local shopkeepers are often extremely obliging and will willingly take time to show children a little about their trade. Observational drawing is an excellent way to help children look carefully at buildings, and their work can be amazingly detailed. Within the school there may well be apparatus in forgotten corners or cupboards that can be used appropriately in the modern curriculum. Some things become obsolete, for example maps of the USSR or pictures of 'An African Village' or 'Shipbuilding on the Clyde'. Other things are still useful, such as a chart showing the life cycle of a butterfly, or a model skeleton.

Practising skills

Many people feel that, if there has been a decline in reading standards in recent years, this is partly due to the very broad curriculum that is now a statutory requirement. The '3 Rs' used to take up by far the largest amount of time in a primary day. Now there also has to be space for science, technology, information technology, history, geography, music, art, games, drama. It may not be hard to find the time for instructing in these areas, but it is hard to find the time for practising the new skills. The Victorians taught their children to have beautiful handwriting not because they had an infallible system of teaching, but because the children practised and practised in a way that we would find unacceptably tedious today. Victorian society depended on a huge pool of clerical workers to do all the office jobs that are now done by computers and word-processors.

Yet teachers should not be afraid of giving the children repetitive practice in areas which they consider fundamentally important in our society today, for example the immediate recall of number bonds, or working with units of measurement. Employers often complain that their youngest recruits have to be trained to do the simplest calculation when they first start their jobs. The breadth of the curriculum certainly makes the practice harder, as there is such a pressure of time; the rationale, however, is that it gives children skills that they will be able to use for the rest of their lives.

There are ways of giving the children experiences in music and drama for instance that are fairly intensive over a short time, but do not figure in the timetable on a regular basis. This may be the way in which to create more practice time. Many schools run Book Weeks and Maths Weeks, when the emphasis is only on the one subject. Other schools plan a 'whole school topic' at some point in the year. If, for example, the topic was 'The Sea,' then mixed age-groups could be made up to engage in various activities connected with the sea. Activities could include some drama about a voyage, learning songs of the sea, learning how to put up a sail in a real dinghy (provided by some obliging parents?), writing poems, looking at real fish and painting them, plotting famous voyages on maps, hearing stories about the sea, and making some models of boats or a lighthouse. A week spent in this way can give an impetus to teaching and learning throughout the school, and is well worth the effort of organising it.

Reflection

We all need time to reflect on what we have been told. This is the process by which we internalise the new information and make it our own. Reflection is often done best when we have a fairly simple concrete task to do with our hands, and at the same time allow our minds to play with the subject we are studying. Children need this time to be built in to any learning process, and it is easy to set up activities which will provide this space. In classes you will often find children being asked to put bits of text in order (sequencing), or discussing what words will best fit in to gaps in a text (Cloze procedure). Both these strategies are good ways of getting the children to go over information that they have received firstly from the class teacher. Discussions, either formal or informal, are also valuable for providing opportunities for reflection. You will often find that investigations, problem-solving, model-making and painting give the children the chance to talk over what they have been thinking about.

Signposting

The differentiated day should always give children something to look forward to. Coming together, as a class, splitting into groups, or working with a friend at different times of the day gives variety. Finishing a group work session early enough to bring the class together again before break could give time for children to perform a little play, or read some of their work to the others. Or it may give you time to explain about the timetable for the next part of the day, or give an introduction to a video you want them to watch. This signposting is a very important part of providing the children with enough clues to know what is expected of them, giving them a greater sense of purpose and preventing confusion.

Another way of using signposting is to consider ways of making the routine work in your classroom sound exciting by signposting the activities with your own titles. For example, practice in learning number bonds or tables facts can be called something special like 'Number Trail', and the children can be motivated by working daily on what is essentially a routine task of learning certain number facts. If you provide some apparatus to go with this daily session, for example a display or special coloured paper to work on, the children will be motivated even more. Children are very easily encouraged to work by an imaginative teacher who can make the most mundane task seem fresh.

The whole classroom environment should also provide the children with ample physical signposting, so that they can collect what they need for their work without bothering the teacher. Many teachers plan the room with this in mind, and you will probably see good examples as you visit schools. Every area of the room can encourage the children to work independently when necessary. By labelling areas for specific activities, for example a 'listening corner' or a 'craft area', you are indicating that the room is a workshop and there is an appropriate method of working in each area. Signs such as 'Three children can play with the sand' or 'Natural History Reference Books' also indicate that you have everything under control, and you expect the children to work in a similarly controlled way.

Adult helpers

When other adults come into the classroom to help they are often asked to supervise a group, or perhaps sit with one child and help with reading or writing. Some of these adults may be paid non-teaching assistants who are employed to work alongside a specific child as part of that child's educational provision. Others will be unpaid helpers, recruited from the children's families, who are interested in the school and want to volunteer their services in any way. Dads and grandads are more frequently seen in schools now, since unemployment has become so widespread. It is very difficult for student teachers to feel they have the 'right' to tell anyone else what to do, and it is also hard to feel they are being watched as they teach their first sessions. But all adult help is valuable in the classroom, and students will have to prepare for their help in the same way as they prepare for the children, so they know exactly how helpers will be deployed for each session. In some sessions the adult could provide reading or writing support for a few children. In other sessions, when you are giving a class lesson for example, the adult could be asked to make apparatus, or cut paper, or tidy shelves. It is most useful if you can find out what particular strengths each helper has. In this way you can make the most of them. People are very diffident about admitting their skills and it is all too easy to miss the chance of some expert help in something. However, the helping adults will not mind being asked to do menial jobs, as they can see that housekeeping is a major part of a well-run classroom, and the teacher is better employed in teaching and preparation than in cleaning paint-brushes.

Summary

In this chapter the organisation of the teaching day has been considered. The implications of the National Curriculum mean that the concepts, knowledge and skills of every subject need to be included in the teacher's planning. Methods of teaching need to be considered that are fit for the purpose. This means that the skills of class, group and individual teaching should be used by every teacher. This chapter has also considered the importance of novelty and routine, reflection, coherence, progression, signposting, and the place of adult helpers.

CHAPTER 4

What does Talk do?

Talk has a chapter to itself because it leads everywhere else. If you ask a child 'What does talk do?' he or she might well say 'Makes my teacher cross', and so it does when chattering takes the place of learning. There is no point in writing idealistically about the importance of talk without acknowledging that school is the centre of children's social life, and, just like us, they love to talk to their friends. In order to make the best use of talk, we should welcome the fact that the children are uninhibited and vocal, and take steps to use this for the benefit of their learning as well as their enjoyment. The silent classroom is rare, and does not often signal a happy place.

The National Curriculum

The National Curriculum has marked the importance of talking and listening, making them the first Attainment Target in the English curriculum. It also stresses that talk can be a means of communication and a tool for learning in every primary subject. For it is from talk that all else follows. From talking children can be encouraged to read, to tell stories and poems, to role-play and act in dramatic presentations, to write through discussion and editing, to debate, to come to scientific and mathematical conclusions, to make historical and geographical discoveries, to find technological solutions, to achieve artistic satisfaction, and to grow up. You can help them to use talk in all its forms, but fortunately you do not have to teach them how to talk. This is the amazing language acquisition that they have already gained in the first few years of their lives. You can work with this language knowledge, which usually includes a complete understanding of grammar and a vocabulary of several thousand words by the age of five. There will be variations in the development of children's oral language, and children who are learning English as a second language will obviously be less advanced. But by and large the child entering school is a language user with a great resource that teachers can draw on. This provides a valuable link with home learning, for it is the oral mode which children have been using before they enter school. Talk is also a crucial part of the development of thought. Is it possible to think without language? Many philosophers think not, or at least only in a very restricted way, and therefore feel that as we increase our vocabulary and our sophistication of speech we are mirroring our growing sophistication of thought.

The first Attainment Target in English is called 'Speaking and Listening' which indicates that there has to be a listener for every talker, and that listening can be fostered in different contexts in the same way as talking. The Programmes of Study for the first two Key Stages include suggestions for what could be seen as 'speaking' activities, such as story-telling and more formal tasks, and 'talking' activities, such as expressing opinions and recounting events. There is an emphasis on working in groups collaboratively, and on using the whole curriculum to encourage talking and listening skills.

Oracy

In chapter 1 there were some examples which showed that children can provide all-important clues to their learning by what they say. It was suggested that the teacher who listens is able to make useful notes in her mind about each child. Talk is a window into the minds of children. It is all the more surprising, therefore, that, historically, talk has been ignored as part of the learning process. In the traditional classroom, children were expected to be silent while the teacher talked.

Andrew Wilkinson (1965) coined the word 'oracy' in an attempt to raise the status of talk. Later, secondary schools began to include oral testing as part of the GCSE exams, and this made teachers analyse their methods of using talk in their sessions, mainly in English lessons. Recently, starting in 1988, there has been a National Oracy Project which has worked to spread ideas from innovative teachers to others who want to build talk into their teaching. Now there are many books available which back up the National Curriculum specifics on talk. Here we can only provide a short introduction to the subject.

Children at home

Young children at home first learn to talk by imitation of the people around them. From the first noises a baby makes to a person leaning over the cot, there is the aim to communicate and make meaning. Gradually children try to make sounds more like those they hear. The human brain seems to have a built-in ability to pick out the most significant parts of any utterance and begin to use them to make embryonic sentences. So a child will say 'car gone' or 'Teddy down' to mark a variety of happenings. Mothers and other close carers are adept at interpreting these small remarks, and expanding them for the child to listen to and eventually learn. Another trait which is part of the early language learning of every child is the ability to instigate dialogues and demand attention from the carer. Parents may think they are choosing to talk to the child, but in fact it is the child who asks for, and gets, the attention.

First steps at school

This language learning continues in the classroom, although the ratio of children to adults immediately raises some problems. No teacher can give a single child the amount of attention received at home during the first few years of life. Barbara Tizard (Tizard and Hughes 1984) researched children's talk in playgroups and found some disturbing evidence. The children who had been active in questioning and learning language at home became quiet in the playgroups when they found there were fewer adults to relate to. Instead of endlessly questioning 'Why Mummy?', they simply answered the questions which adults put to them, surely a less efficient way of learning. Similarly, Gordon Wells (1986), in his long study of children's early language acquisition in Bristol, found that teachers who were not prepared to listen to children attempting to make their own meanings often discouraged further efforts:

> In early education, it is an oft-repeated slogan that one should start from where the child is – not where a child of a given age from a given background can be expected to be, but where each individual child is. And what better way of knowing where they are than by listening to what they have to say; by attending, in the tasks that they engage in, to

the meanings that they make. Of course this is not the end of effective teaching, but it is an essential beginning – and not only at the beginning of the year, but in each new interaction. Only on this basis is it possible to negotiate challenges that will extend children's control and understanding that are mutually relevant.
(Gordon Wells 1986, p.101)

Observing

As a student, you will have chances of observing children's talk in the classroom in a way that is hard for a working teacher. As you sit at the side of children during their discussions about their work, you will begin to notice many characteristics of their interactions. There may be children who dominate others, and children who are very diffident about offering any opinion. Some children may be good at expressing their ideas verbally, but slow to write them down, and you may find that you are acting as a 'scribe' for these children in an attempt to give them the satisfaction of seeing their ideas translated into print. Your intervention in this way might be the motivation that the child needs to become a more independent writer.

You may also notice that children with a home language which is not English talk to one another in that language. The benefits of this are enormous. Children who are meeting new concepts in, say, maths, will be helped if they can use their first language to explore the idea. To have to translate these new thoughts into English at the same time as encountering them for the first time is to overload the brain. Unfortunately, many children with non-English home languages get the idea that 'school' means English, and they become quite embarrassed about their own language unless there is positive encouragement from the school. A good primary school will try to involve parents and other visitors who speak different languages to take part in the classroom life, and there will be displays and discussions on the variety of written languages. It is vitally important not to cut children off from the culture of their first few years, for this is their birthright, and language is one of the most significant ways in which we learn our own identity.

During periods of observation, you may begin to notice what factors make for a successful class attitude to talk. The classes which function best have the children working together with greater autonomy, referring to each other when necessary, and focussed purposefully on their work. This independence can mask the amount of work the experienced teacher has put in to the class to establish the ground rules of talk, and it is worthwhile trying to pin-point exactly what the teacher has done during her time with the class. Conversely, you may find that you are observing in a class which does not use talk to good purpose, and be able to analyse what is missing from the working atmosphere. Whatever type of class you are in, and whatever the age of the children, there is always plenty to be learned from observing the routines and the ethos, and trying to analyse why things are as they are. The process of establishing a certain atmosphere in the school and the separate classrooms is often called the 'hidden agenda'.

Planning for talk

Most school activities involve talk. It is the teacher's job to identify what purpose the talk should serve, and to help the children understand this purpose. There will have to be planning in both these areas. The second area, that of making the children aware of how to behave in different talk situations, will become more important as the children get older, and the range of talk becomes larger.

In simple terms, talk can be seen to have three aspects, all of which are used together in collaborative learning. Firstly, there is the social skill of interacting with others. Teaching this is one of the main jobs of any reception class, where children have to learn to live as part of a group, to take turns at speaking, and to listen to others. Social opportunities are provided in the room with dressing-up clothes and construction toys, and so on. The second purpose of talk is to communicate with others. The making of meaning has to be clear enough for the listener to understand. For some children this strand of talk may have to involve speech therapy, but for the majority, there will be a steady development of clarity and a broadening vocabulary to cope with the most demanding messages that need transmitting. Similarly, the listening ability of the children will grow, so that they can understand longer and more complicated stories, instruction and explanations. The third strand is that of cognitive development, which is obviously linked with the first two aspects of talk. Here, the child is using language to formulate thought and this can be seen in the monologues of infant children as they play. They are developing their own understanding by translating and refining their thoughts into an ever-increasing variety of words, and rehearsing these words to themselves out loud, for the pleasure of hearing their thoughts. Later this talk becomes internalised, but still continues, and is a vital part of learning.

When planning to integrate talk into the work in the classroom, in any of the aspects mentioned above, remember that it will take time. It is very easy to cut talk-time down to a brief minute or two because of an anxiety to 'get on' with a task which will produce something concrete by the end of the session. But making a decision to allow time for talk will pay enormous dividends. Not only will it help children to clarify and expand their thoughts, it will also, if you make your plans overt and involve the children in laying down the rules for talk, give them a voice in the organisation of their work. Many problems, from tidying up to unfriendliness between children, can be solved by discussions which assume that the opinions of the children are valued. Children who feel valued will respond by showing their most mature side, and the whole ethos of the classroom will reflect your decision to make the most of talk.

This is a list of rules that a year 6 class decided on. You can hear the authentic voice of the children as you read the list. They are well aware of the factors that disrupt learning, and in this exercise they are invited to take responsibility for their own behaviour.

1. Make sure everybody takes part.
2. Make sure everybody co-operates.
3. If you disagree, then compromise.
4. Everybody must help each other work as a team.
5. Do not be selfish.
6. Do not interrupt.
7. Listen to everybody's ideas.
8. Do not be silly.
9. Try your hardest.
10. Try not to get upset and sulk.
11. Try not to rush your work.
12. Make your work neat and tidy.
13. Do not laugh at other people's ideas.
14 Only talk about your work.

Planning for talk requires thinking about the activities of the children in a different way. Some examples will help. If a group is going to make a model, the first activity could be to discuss what materials will be needed. Perhaps a plan of the model could be made, with instructions written on it. After this, the group could explain to the rest of the class exactly what they are planning. This preparatory thinking, together with the explanations children give to each other and the class as a whole, has helped to clarify the process in the minds of the children. When the model-making takes place, it will be more purposeful and successful. Another example is the organising of an interview. Perhaps a visitor is coming to the classroom with some specialised experience or knowledge. Instead of asking him or her to talk to the children and then asking for questions at the end, you could ask the children to devise questions in advance. Discussion about useful areas of questioning will focus the children's minds on the subject so that they are more receptive to the visitor.

Kinds of talk

There are many reasons for talk and many types of talk. For example, some talk encourages us to think back into the past (remembering, telling, describing), and some looks to the future (predicting, exploring). Some talk uses the intellect logically (reporting, comparing, persuading), and some talk uses the emotions (personal aspirations, imaginative projections, interpretations). Different types of talk are appropriate to different types of thinking. A good teacher demands that the children expand their repertoire of talk as they get older and pursues the new possibilities this creates. Keeping the repertoire of talk as wide as possible will ensure the children are developing their thoughts at the same time. The Programmes of Study in the National Curriculum are a good guide to the possibilities of talk activities.

Dialect and accent

Teachers also invariably have to consider the tricky subject of dialect and accent. Children bring to school the language they have learned at home. To criticise this is to infer that there is something wrong with their background, and to devalue the children themselves. The English have a great snobbery concerned with certain, but not all, regional dialects. Teachers have to ask themselves about their own values here and ensure that they are positive in their approach to children's spoken language at all times. When the spoken comes to be turned into formal writing, then some variations that are dialectically correct, but formally incorrect, have to be modified, but this is not always the case in other forms of writing. It is important that children should be able to write standard English by the age of, say, nine or ten, but this does not mean their dialect variations should be considered wrong from the age of five. This is a very emotive and confused area of debate, and teachers have to tread a careful path between criticising a child's language too harshly at too young an age, and denying the child's entitlement to knowledge of the correct forms of spoken and written English.

Your own talk

If you have the chance to tape yourself working with a group of children you may well be appalled when you hear yourself. It is a common revelation to find that, as teachers, we talk far too much, interrupting and paraphrasing what the children say when there is no need to say anything. Teachers who worked with the National Oracy Project found exactly this, and made a conscious effort to keep quiet during discussions. This meant that at times there were silent gaps in the discussion, when the children were thinking, but the responses that followed these gaps were far longer and more self-assured. Our training makes us feel that we must set the agenda all the time, and instigate all that goes on in the discussion. Children will look to us to do this, and merely answer our questions unless we show them that we expect a more egalitarian form of talk in which they are allowed to question and answer.

It is a good thing to remember that nothing breeds success more than success. An encouraging remark will help a child say more, and a word of praise is never wasted. Young children especially seem to need constant praise. It is salutary to think back to one's own school-days, and remember the teachers who gave praise or made encouraging noises and remarks, and the ones who gave criticism as a means of encouraging work. There is no doubt which style produced the best results, and it will be the same in your own classroom. Little phrases like, 'Can you tell me more', 'Yes, go on', 'Explain this to me again', and even 'Mm . . .' will all help the child to be more articulate and to feel that his or her contribution is valued. Treating talk as an important part of the curriculum will show children that they too have a

40

responsibility to play their part in discussions in a sensible way. You set the tone, with comments like 'We've heard several interesting views in favour; now, is there anyone who would like to put a different view?'

Development in thought (cognitive development) means that there is a need for a developing vocabulary. Teachers should be clear about the precise meaning of words introduced as part of maths or science work, for example. When children are using a word for the first time they often get it slightly wrong. This process is very like the early stages of speech learning when they said 'bikkit' for biscuit for a few weeks. Now they are unsure of the meaning, and the teacher has to allow time for plenty of practice. An example could be the terms for four-sided shapes. A square is a special quadrilateral, but a quadrilateral is not always a square. Explanations from the teacher are useful, but the children will understand best by using the words frequently themselves in conversation with others.

Summary

This chapter has given an introduction to the place of talk in the curriculum, and how encouraging purposeful talk can affect both the learning and the hidden agenda of the class. There is also some discussion about the place of teacher talk. The issue of dialect speaking is briefly considered.

CHAPTER 5

Support for Reading and Writing in Key Stage 1

> Pupils should encounter an environment in which they are surrounded by books and other reading material presented in an attractive and inviting way.
>
> (National Curriculum Programme of Study for Reading, Key Stage 1)

In this chapter the hugely important subject of teaching reading and writing will be explored. Because this is so central to primary teaching, there is another chapter following which continues the subject in more detail, with the emphasis on the older children working on Key Stage 2. You may notice, when observing in schools, that the teaching of reading and writing is of first importance in infant rooms, but not so marked in many junior rooms. For some children, there is a need to continue this emphasis right through the primary years, and these chapters will give you a grounding in how this might be achieved.

Methods of teaching reading

Many students complain that they are not taught how to teach reading, but just shown various suggestions and materials and told to get on with it. When they get into schools they find many different methods and mixtures of methods, and this confuses them further. There is no doubt that the teaching of reading has been beset with fads and fashions for the last twenty years, and sometimes these have not been properly understood and implemented by the schools who adopted them. One strand of reading behaviour has often been emphasised at the expense of others.

The method which sounds the most scientific is the phonic method. The reasoning is that if a child learns all the letter sounds first, he or she can 'sound out' any word in a book. This works for some words of course, like d-o-g, but it doesn't work for other equally common words like g-o-e-s, unless you also learn a collection of spelling rules (and exceptions to those rules) at the same time, which would be far too difficult for a five-year-old. This led to the devising of tedious reading primers which avoided irregular words, and gave children contrived sentences like 'The cat ran to the pot and sat in it.' Some books even hyphenated multisyllabled words to help this sounding-out process, giving children the puzzle of reading that 'mot-her is sit-ting in the garden'.

The 'Look and Say' or whole word method appeared as a great step forward. Now children were invited to learn the whole word as a recognisable shape, and not to worry about the individual sounds of the letters which can be so misleading in out spelling system. This method worked best when children were given books with a controlled and limited vocabulary, and the method became the basis of many reading schemes in the sixties and seventies. Children could recognise high interest words like 'aeroplane' and 'elephant' without any bother, and stories became more interesting as a result. As well as high interest words, there was a growing awareness of another class of words, the high frequency words (also known as 'key words'). These are the little words like 'the', 'and', 'is' 'are', 'he', 'it', 'in', and 'goes', that make up a large proportion of all texts. Learning these words is hard because they are so abstract and difficult to illustrate, but instant recognition is one of the keys to fluent reading so practising them is a very worthwhile exercise. The vocabulary for each book in a graded series was learned by using flash cards, and then the book was given to the child to read with success.

Many reading schemes were devised which relied on one or other of these methods, or a mixture. Teachers often knew instinctively when their classes were in need of more phonic work or in need of more contextual clues to help them read, and adapted the school 'scheme' as they saw fit. Others saw the need to link reading with writing, and encouraged children to write their own stories which were then used as reading materials.

It is unfortunately true that 'there is no one method, medium, approach, device, or philosophy that holds the key to the process of learning to read' (Bullock Report, para 6.1). It is also true that reading is complex, and to divide up the skills needed and teach them separately does not make the child a fluent reader. However, you need to understand what these skills are, and to ensure that you give the children practice in them as you prepare your reading and writing programmes of work. Both the phonic approach and the 'Look and Say' method have been questioned as methods that exclude all other teaching, but that is not to say that the ideas behind them are to be ignored. Rather, they are to be incorporated into an up-to-date synthesis of reading methods which takes into account the child's oral language development and the motivation to read and write which comes from wanting to communicate. The concept of phonics is an important part of learning to spell, while the recognition of whole words is crucial for reading at a speed that promotes understanding.

The making of meaning

The main point to remember when teaching a child to read is the aim to make meaning from the text. This is what children have been doing ever since they first pointed to a teddy in a rag book when they were in their prams. They realised then that the world of reality (or the world of fantasy) could be represented on a flat surface which could be held in the hand. This is the true meaning of a book. All the reading activities which are introduced to children in school should be built on this inherent truth. The meaning that books contain is there to be shared, even when the children cannot read the text themselves. This story-telling aspect of sharing books has been shown to be of tremendous importance. The child who has plenty of bedtime stories at home, and daytime book-sharing sessions too, is the child who is well-prepared to become an independent user of books later on (Meek 1982, chapter 2).

Students are often asked to prepare a story to share with a group of children as part of their early work in the classroom. This is an ideal chance for you to find out, if you do not already have experience, just how powerful a good book and a good story-teller can be. The children's involvement and comments are usually a delight, and you will find yourself enjoying the session much more that you anticipated. The natural question that you as a teacher will ask yourself is, how do I use this enthusiasm for 'story' to make readers?

What to read

So what are the requirements for making readers? The first necessity is for good books for the children to use. It was the search for these books that led teachers to adopt the 'real books' approach to reading. All this silly term means is that teachers were no longer satisfied with giving children rather tedious 'reading scheme' books, with banal plots and no literary merit. Instead, they looked at the whole range of children's fiction and non-fiction to find books of a suitable level for each child. Authors and illustrators with flair are able to get into the hearts of the children. The text of the book becomes learned without effort, and thus the child becomes a reader. Books such as *Rosie's Walk* by Pat Hutchins have become classics in their own time, by providing a simple text, which, combined with the pictures, tells an ironic story that appeals to the young readers. Other books, like *I'm Coming to get You* by Tony Ross and *Where the Wild Things Are* by Maurice Sendak, explore the fears of children and gently reassure them that all will be well. It was this centrality of subject matter which was felt to be lacking in the bland 'readers' of some of the schemes that were available a few years ago. You may find examples of these older reading schemes in schools that you visit. Have a look at them and see if you think they are good enough to offer young beginner readers.

Now things have changed for the better. The latest reading schemes have been produced as a result of the move towards 'real books'. The publishers have understood the need to provide variety, and plots that speak to children. Good authors and illustrators have been commissioned, and well-researched teachers' books provide excellent suggestions for using the materials. Now, many schools are pleased to make use of these schemes, as they know they will provide good basic reading material, with graded and limited vocabulary, but not at the expense of story. If the teachers' books are used properly, they will provide a thorough reading curriculum which encourages children to use all the clues to reading that they can find. These 'clues' will be discussed fully in the next section of this chapter. As you go into schools, it will be well worth getting to know some of the most common schemes in use today, such as Oxford Reading Tree, Storychest, Sunshine, Red-Nose Readers, Longman's Reading World and Ginn.

You may find that the schools you visit operate a 'colour coding' system for their stock of reading books. Coloured stickers are used to grade the books according to reading difficulty. This is usually done by the teacher with special responsibility for English. The difficulty of the book is said to be its 'readability' and this is decided by looking at the vocabulary, sentence length and structure, size of typeface, illustrations, and the arrangement of the text on the page. Several reading experts have worked out formulas for readability, but the best-known index in this country is the one by Cliff Moon (Moon 1992). The children can then read from a particular band of books and tackle a wide range of typefaces and formats. On the other hand, the risk is that children will not have enough exposure to the same words written in the same typeface to be able to learn them thoroughly. Schools, therefore, have to make sure they have sessions on word and letter learning as well as book reading.

The second requirement for encouraging reading is to make reading part of the whole literacy programme. The importance of linking reading to writing has already been mentioned. Many schools understand that a five-year-old child is a very self-centred little person who responds best when reading material is very close to his or her heart. For this reason, the school may use the child's speech to make the first reading material. So if the child reports that he has made a model aeroplane with his auntie, then this is written and copied by the child, and put into a book that becomes the 'reading book' for a week or so. The ownership of these little books is a great source of pride, and reading becomes a very personal sharing of meaning. The National Curriculum includes this important way of making early reading materials in its Programme of Study for reading in Key Stage 1: 'Pupils' own writing – either independently written, or stories dictated to the teacher or composed in collaboration with other pupils – should form part of the resources for reading.'

You may find that the 'Breakthrough to Literacy' method of composing these books is used. Children collect their own folder full of words that they need to write their own stories and messages, and put these words into a plastic holder for copying. The Breakthrough system is committed to using the children's own language for their first reading and written work, and it is well worth investigating further. The materials are available in many infant classroooms, together with the teachers' handbook. (Mackay, Thompson, Schaub 1978).

Clues for reading

The third requirement is for children to be encouraged to look closely at books and print. In the years before they come to school, children have had many opportunities to see what reading is for. They understand, to a greater or lesser extent, depending on their home experiences, that reading gives you information, tells you stories, labels things and is generally a very important part of life. They know from the context of the writing what message it will probably contain, and often play at being bus conductors with tickets, or doctors with prescriptions. They have also learned how a book works: that is to say they can pick one up and study it by turning the pages. Marie Clay designed tests for emerging readers (called *Sand* and *Stones*) which are useful for finding out how much children know about books (Clay 1972). For example, does a child know which is the writing and which is the picture? Does he or she know where the first page of the story is? Now that schools have to test seven-year-olds it is interesting to get some 'baseline tests' done as soon as children enter school. This is the only way of assessing how much children have progressed.

Teachers carry on this teaching about the significance of books and print. The reception class has many opportunities for continuing the kind of play that the children engage in at home and at playgroup. The class teacher will also encourage children to look at books and share them with friends and other adults. There may also be a selection of 'Big Books'. These are much bigger than normal, and specially designed to be used with groups of children. The teacher, as she tells the story, points to the words with her finger, and turns the pages, carefully modelling what a reader does. She notes the features of the print, such as the capital letters for names, the full stops at the ends of sentences and perhaps the initial sounds of some of the words. In this way much phonic teaching can be done within the framework of story-telling. Of course, it is quite possible to have a story-book with no text at all. The story can still be told collaboratively from the pictures. The meaning is made and the experience is shared. 'Big Books' are part of the materials for all the most recent reading schemes, and are invaluable. They are often copies of normal-sized books, which the children can then take home and reread. Some 'Big Books' are not story-books, but intended to stimulate discussion and writing. You could use a 'Big Book', or make your own, for a story session in a reception class.

For early readers, context is all important, as has been mentioned. They can 'read' a birthday card, telling you that it says 'Happy Birthday'. Similarly, they can confidently read labels around the room which are stuck to various pieces of apparatus and furniture. Some teachers take advantage of this, and label things with phrases and sentences rather than with nouns alone. For example, an aquarium could say 'Fish', or it could say 'There are four fish in here.' An infant room provides lots of opportunity for displaying a large vocabulary in this way, and the words and phrases can not only be read, but 'borrowed' for writing purposes. Useful phrases include 'I can see', 'I like', 'We all go to. . .', ' . . . in the box', 'under the table', and so on. The room becomes a reading and writing resource, leading the children easily into the idea of using simple dictionaries for writing, and, of course, to books for reading. In books, the context is often supplied by the pictures, which is why the illustrator's talent is so essential.

Phonic awareness

However irregular our English spelling, there is still an important correspondence between the look of the words and their sound. This is known as the grapho-phonic connection. Teachers have always tried to make this link apparent to children, so they can begin to make guesses about the words from the letters contained in the words. Research has shown that children who understand the principle of rhyming are well on the way to understanding reading, and those that don't are going to find reading harder (Bryant and Bradley 1985). This makes sense, because words that rhyme contain a common word-part which is usually spelled the same. For example, 'cat', 'fat', 'rat', and 'mat' all contain '-at'; 'hill', 'fill', 'pill', and 'will' all contain '-ill'. Playing rhyming games with children and singing nursery rhymes will increase their understanding of what rhymes with what, and help them pick out the similarities in words when they begin to look at print. The recognition of word-parts is a valuable tool for reading, although it will not provide an infallible guide to the sound of the word (think of the famous list of 'cough', 'bough', dough', 'enough'). Similarly, teaching about alliteration will help children with initial consonants. Silly sentences or phrases can be taught ('five frantic frogs in frilly frocks'). A teacher who draws childrens attention to word-parts in informal ways is doing more to foster reading than one who teaches letter sounds alone 'D says duh', 'P says puh' is not helpful at all because the 'uh' sound is not present in words that use those consonants.

Moving on

The vast majority of children in years 1 and 2 are going to make great strides with their reading. The ones that do not progress need to be identified at this stage, because they will need very close monitoring from now on. The reasons for their slowness are varied. Perhaps they are learning English as a second language, or perhaps they have missed a lot of school. For others, it may be that their hearing is poor, and they do not pick up differences between words clearly enough for them to make sense of print. Others again may be generally slow in their learning habits, and need patient 'overlearning' at every stage. This means that there must be a lot of repetition in the work these children do. The last small group may have difficulty in distinguishing letter and word shapes, and be rather hazy about the order of letters in their writing. Children who show these symptoms, and yet are obviously intelligent enough to be able to read, are often labelled 'dyslexic' (Hornsby 1988; Pumphrey and Peter 1992). This term has to be used with caution. Only a small proportion of children who find reading difficult will have dyslexia or 'word-blindness', and it is best if this is diagnosed by an expert in special needs. They need a careful programme of literacy, with the emphasis on 'little and often' in the tasks they are asked to do. They will have to learn words and word-parts in a more deliberate way than the usual beginner reader, because their perception of the words is not so sharp. Nevertheless, they should not be given a diet of words to learn in a list all the time. They, too, need the enjoyment of books and the stories they contain. For they, just like all the children in the class, want to become readers. It is often a great frustration to them that they cannot 'crack the code' as they see others doing.

Early readers need lots of practice. In most schools the children take their reading book home every night. During the school day they may read to the teacher or to another adult, or share a book with a friend. Some schools organise a 'reading buddy' scheme, where older children meet younger children for a session each week, and the older one listens and comments on the younger one's reading. This is usually very successful and leads to friendships that might not normally develop. The class teacher has the time-consuming but essential task of keeping track of what each child is reading, and how they are progressing. Records are kept up to date by giving each child a book in which parents and teacher comment every time the child reads. This record can then be used when completing the more formal records, and the parents are sometimes invited to the school to be shown how to join in the reading experience in the best possible way. They are encouraged to make teaching sessions enjoyable, by sitting comfortably close to their child, reading the book together rather than expecting the child to be able to read everything, and giving lots of praise. Some schools produce booklets that give this advice. The terms 'paired reading' or 'shared reading' are often used to describe these reading activities. Reading is seen as a joint venture between school and home, and the beginner reader is given every encouragement to make the most of his growing abilities. Just as the apprentice swimmer is not thrown into the pool to manage without help, so the apprentice reader is given help and encouraged to make the most of increasing skills (Waterland 1985).

Hearing reading

It is interesting to realise that when a teacher 'hears' a child read, she is asking the child to perform a task that will eventually be redundant. The fluent reader does not read aloud, but carries the message of the print straight from the page into his or her brain. As children get more fluent they reflect this redundancy in reading aloud, and often say to the teacher that they can read faster when they read alone. But in the early stages, the sharing of a book with the teacher is the only way to monitor the child's understanding and progress in reading.

Hearing reading takes up a good deal of time. This is why parents and other adult helpers are often recruited. The teacher has to be sure that all the rest of the class are busy and can be left before she devotes herself to one child. This time is precious. The most important thing to do with it is to reassure the child that he or she is reading successfully. There should never be a hint of 'failure' from a reading session. The atmosphere should be sociable and intimate as you discuss the book and its story. When children read you should help them with words that cannot be read, or ask them to look at the picture again for another clue (Meek 1982, chapter 3).

As children read individually you should be noting their 'miscues'. These are the evidence of their reading ability. Are they substituting a similar word ('house' for 'home' for example) which does not change the sense? This is a positive error, and a hopeful sign that they will soon be reading 'home'. Or are they substituting a word which does not make sense (horse for house)? This would mean they are not thinking about the sense of the story but only about the words. Are they hesitating over words that are similar ('the', 'these', 'then', 'that')? If they are, it may be they are only looking at the beginning of words, and need to be shown how to look right to the end of the words before saying them. Knowledge of letter sounds is helpful, but they may be relying on it too much, and trying to 'sound out' every word. Maybe they should have some practice in whole word recognition. They may well reverse some words ('was' for 'saw'). This is a very common miscue in early reading. As you listen to them you may be making a few notes. These will be very helpful, not only for your record-keeping and report-writing, but in order to plan work for each particular child. A thorough study of a child's reading in this way is called a 'miscue analysis' and it involves marking a copy of the passage that he or she has read with symbols to show the pattern of their miscues (Goodman, Watson and Burke 1987). It is a useful diagnostic aid. You may find it too time-consuming to do such a formal check on every child, but the principles of miscue analysis should help you pin-point the help that the child needs.

Support for writing

Writing and reading, together with talking, are all interwoven in early literacy teaching, but there are things that a teacher can do specifically to support writing at the early stages. Most children believe that they can write when they come to school. They have been using their 'scribble' writing in their games for several years. Teachers have to build on this confidence rather than remove it by insisting that all writing is accurate. The National Curriculum makes a point of saying that children should be able to compose at greater length than they are capable of writing on their own. This is a recognition that children both want and need to tell stories and anecdotes that can be produced in print. Some schools encourage children to write on their own, knowing that the accuracy will slowly improve as the children learn more and more about what words look like. This system has become known as 'emergent writing'; the skills of writing are encouraged to emerge from the 'scribble-writing' just as the skills of speaking emerge from the babble of a two-year-old. Other schools begin to teach writing by 'scribing' for the children, so that their spoken accounts become written for them, and perhaps read by them. This is often done by the teacher after they have drawn a picture, and can be transferred straight on to the computer. The 'Breakthrough to Literacy' method has already been mentioned. This again makes use of the children's own language to create written messages and stories. These methods of producing writing are much more alive for the children than merely copying a sentence that the teacher has made up for the class. Another way of encouraging children to write is to tell them to just put the initial letter of words they do not know, and draw a line to indicate the word. The teacher can fill in the missing letters which the child can then copy in the second draft of the text.

Children need to be shown that words are fun and easy to use both in reading and writing. Spelling is a visual skill and children need to look hard at words. By playing with words out of text the teacher can show their patterns and constructions. It is important to be clear about the purpose of these strategies: they are not to replace reading texts as the central experience of literacy learning, but they are essential for teaching the predictability of words. Every game or activity needs to have a specific focus. One set of cards might contain the names of the months of the year which the children can sequence. Another game may ask the children to put words into families, that is to say those words which contain the same letter string. Another box might contain an alphabetical list of words that are specific to the topic being studied.

Reading and writing corners

The importance of making the classroom a resource for reading and writing has already been mentioned. However inadequate the space, it is usually possible to make both reading and writing corners in the room. The writing corner can be a place where there are various pencils and papers to write on. There can also be some games to play, such as those mentioned above, or rhyming dominoes or matching words to pictures. A computer gives the children the chance to write their text on to the screen, where it can be edited later and printed out. A reading corner can contain the class stock of fiction, with some cushions to give an invitation to children to spend some time with a book. The idea of learning to read and write is very exciting to children, and the classroom should encourage this excitement.

52

Summary

This chapter emphasises that children's early attempts at reading and writing are for the same purpose as an adult's, that is to make meaning. Teachers have to provide support for the emergent skills of the learner, and must on no account take away the belief that the child can read and write. Historically, various methods of teaching reading have been used and this chapter considers the best combination of methods for use today. The importance of clues (pictures, phonic, context) is emphasised, and the need to record and assess 'miscues' is explained.

CHAPTER 6

Processes of Reading and Writing in Key Stage 2

Pupils should read an increasingly wide range and variety of texts in order to become more experienced readers.
(National Curriculum Programme of Study for Reading, Key Stage 2)

Writing is a way of preserving things, or as I say to the children, it's like making a photo album. Of course it's not the only way to preserve things because memory is a preserver, video and sound tape are too. But there are unique features about writing as a preserver. The process of recording is actually quite slow, but it is cheap and portable. When the writing concerned is personal, it has the potential of putting the writer centre-stage
(Michael Rosen 1989 p.24)

The last chapter focussed on the early stages of learning to read and write. After two or three years in the infant classes, most children have gained independence in both reading and writing, and are ready to extend their skills in the junior years. An average child reader of seven is said to have a 'reading age' of seven. They can read appropriate story books quite fluently, but they are by no means able to use this skill with all texts. It is crucially important that direct reading and writing teaching continues at this point, or children will not learn the full repertoire of reading and writing skills. It is these skills that will be discussed in this chapter.

When teaching was more formal and didactic, the emphasis in both reading and writing teaching was to give the children a body of knowledge. Each part of this knowledge was practised through exercises, and the child who could 'do' these exercises (comprehension, dictation, punctuation, spelling), was pronounced literate. Writing anything personal or imaginative was called 'creative writing' and occupied one period a week at the most. Reading was done from a 'reading book'. Reading for research was unheard of, and reading for enjoyment was something to be done at home.

Things changed. The child-centred approach to primary teaching in the sixties and seventies showed that children's intellectual development is just one facet of their total personality. Emotional and psychological development is continuing at the same time, and must be taken into account when teaching. It became generally understood that progress in literacy was dependent on motivation and understanding, and that this did not come from exercises. Books and materials took on a friendlier style, and the children's home culture and their interest in such things as sport and television programmes was acknowledged.

In the eighties there was a further interest in the kinds of literacy tasks that children engaged in at school. The purpose of each task was now seen as crucial to its fulfilment. When children discussed and understood why they were writing a piece, and who the intended audience was going to be, they had a far clearer concept of what kind of writing was expected of them. Similarly, there was an understanding that children should be shown that there are different ways of reading depending on purpose. A text can be scanned for key words when some research is being done, or read carefully to enjoy the poetic language.

What to read

One of the most fascinating processes to watch in a classroom is the developing reading habits of the children, especially when they are about seven or eight. This is the time when they realise they can move on from books that are obviously 'scheme readers' and begin to choose from the huge selection of children's literature. Some characteristics of the early reading books are still needed. For example, children like quite big print and will reject books with small print at a glance. They are daunted by dense text which is not broken up with conversation or illustration. The plot of books has to be simple, and morality is best understood in rather 'black and white' terms.

This is the secret of success for such authors as Enid Blyton. Adults find it hard to see the attraction of her rather trite and obvious stories, but children devour them as their first 'chapter stories' as one child put it. Rather than disapproving of these books, teachers should recognise that the child who reads three *Famous Five* adventures in one week is practising many skills of story reading that will be further extended in other fiction when the child is ready to move on.

There is a wide variation in the way that schools treat literacy learning. In some schools children read to their teachers in an almost secret way, and nothing more about reading is seen or talked about. In other schools there is a constant celebration of literacy and literature. Activities, events and displays are arranged which draw on the world of written and spoken story for their stimulus, and children are encouraged to read and write for each other, and for as many other audiences as possible. The idea of reading as a performance is not forgotten, nor is the need for children to respond to story with drama, painting and other crafts. Stories to read or to listen to are chosen from the enormous range available: folk tales from Britain and from other countries, fairy tales such as *Rumpelstiltskin*, stories in verse such as Belloc's *Cautionary Tales*, classic novels like Frances Hodgson Burnett's *The Secret Garden*, old favourites like Richmal Crompton's *William* stories, and a varied diet of poetry. Non-fiction is also part of the children's experience, and they are taught the best ways of finding and using information.

Most children of junior age have a reading ability that allows them to step into the exciting world of stories on their own. Teachers need to provide as wide a range of books as possible, and to check that the children are reading with understanding. But there will be some children who want to read 'proper' story-books, but find that they cannot. This disappointment can often cause resentment and an unwillingness to read at all. Publishers are much better nowadays at providing interesting books with easy text, and it really is essential that schools have plenty of these available. Looking at the book while listening to a cassette is another way of providing support for a child who wants to read a book which is too hard for him or her to read independently. There are also easy versions of classic stories which are published by Ladybird and others. Organising sessions with 'reading buddies' can also help the less confident children. Older children are paired with younger ones and they sit and read to each other and talk about their books. The emphasis is on sharing and enjoyment, so that reading is seen as a pleasurable occupation, not a chore or a test.

Reading and writing environment

The last chapter showed how the typical infant classroom is arranged to be an ideal literacy workshop. This should continue in the junior years, adapting the provisions to the more independent work that many of these children can now do. Above all, children in year 3 and above need books of all kinds to satisfy their widening tastes. You will learn to be very critical of books that are just not appropriate. For example, many non-fiction books have wonderful illustrations but a text that is far too difficult. And many story-books written for the seven to nine-year-old age range are printed in a typeface that is too small for the children to feel comfortable with.

Reading and writing corners will still be popular if they are well equipped. Some of the reading and spelling games that children enjoyed in their infant years may have appeal for children who are only now beginning to understand letter patterns and the sound/symbol relationship. Children have an insatiable desire for pencils, paper, rubbers, paper clips, and so on. Equipping a writing table with coloured or decorated paper, or Paddington Bear pencils is a foolproof way of tempting children to write. Tape recorders can be used to record interviews which can then be transcribed. This gives the children an insight into the differences between spoken and written English. Word-processors are very useful for editing work. A pair of children can work together on a piece of text, discussing what changes are needed. The concentration span of the children is growing longer during their junior years, so they need quiet places around the room where they can get down to work without being disturbed.

Writing processes

When you, as a student, first take a small group of children during one of your initial visits to school, there is nothing more satisfying than coming away at the end of the session with a collection of writing that the children have done. It represents the concrete evidence of the session's work, and you can evaluate it at length. But writing is a complex skill, and the developing of it needs careful thought.

Before writing begins there should be time for discussion. The stimulus for writing can be as varied as you can make it, and should if possible include a reason for writing, and a supposed audience. This will indicate the style that is expected. Some writing, for example story writing, is chronological, in that it deals with events through time. Other writing, such as a list or an invitation, is non-chronological. The style of a book review is not the same as the style needed for an adventure story, or for a poem giving an emotional response. As children get older, they have experience of many different kinds of text, and they are able to bring this experience to bear when they do their own writing.

It is often a good idea to separate the compositional aspect of writing from the secretarial. In this way the children are not being asked to concentrate on too many things at once. So a pair of children may work out a dialogue for a puppet play, and jot it down. This is the compositional stage, when they do not need to think about accuracy of spelling or neatness. Later, after rereading and editing this first draft, they can do a neat copy, when the secretarial aspect of writing will be the one to concentrate on. In this way the writing process is made into a much more valuable learning opportunity than if the children were just asked to 'write a puppet play'. Extending the task to include co-operative discussion times and performance times will mean that the children are practising skills across the whole range of literacy attainments (Smith 1982).

Many teachers realise that children are best motivated to write when the subject is close to their heart. But they also have to acknowledge that the curriculum demands that much writing is done for topic work, or for other purposes that may not be so close to the children. For this reason there is quite a widespread use of something known as a 'Writers' Workshop'. A session a week is devoted to the children's own writing. They keep a folder with unfinished work in it, and can choose what they want to write about during this time. The teacher makes herself available as a sympathetic editor, and the children are encouraged to consult each other when they want a second opinion about their work (Graves 1983).

As children develop their literacy skills it is important that the teacher keeps pace with their needs. The National Curriculum gives guidance about what is expected at each level of attainment. Here are two statements of attainment from the writing section, one from level 3 and one from level 4.

Level 3: Begin to revise and redraft in discussion with the teacher, other adults, or other children in the class, paying attention to meaning and clarity as well as checking for matters such as correct and consistent use of tenses and pronouns.

Level 4: Discuss the organisation of their own writing, revise and redraft the writing as appropriate, independently, in the light of that discussion.

You will see from this example that it is not easy to identify a progression here. They key is the word 'independently' in the level 4 statement, and so it is this that the teacher will be looking for to distinguish the child's performance at this level from the level before.

Grammar

Just as children need to know the function of commas and full stops, so they need to understand a little about the way our language is structured. Learning the 'rules of grammar' sounds very dry, but to know the reasons for words to be as they are sounds much more interesting. Think, for example, about the reasons for using an apostrophe. There are two: the first is to show that letters have been missed out and a short form of writing two or more words is being used ('you've' for 'you have', 'I'll' for 'I will', 'shouldn't' for 'should not'); the second is to show ownership, or belonging to, and involves using an 's' as well ('Jill's cat', 'the girl's dog' for one girl and 'the girls' dog' for two or more girls). Using an apostrophe before a simple plural 's' as greengrocers are inclined to do ('potato's', 'apple's') is wrong. This information is quite simple and easy to teach as part of language work in general, and it is essential that children are given explanations like this.

Sometimes the grammar of standard English does not agree with the common spoken form of words. Children who say 'We was up the playing field' have to be shown that there is another formal way of saying and writing this. Teachers have to be tactful: it is unfair to imply that the child's way of speaking is 'wrong'. We also have to be aware of the snobbery that has come to be associated with different regional dialects. A London child's 'we done it' is frowned on much more than a Yorkshire child's 'wait while five minutes' ('while' is used instead of 'until' or 'for' in many places in the north of England). Every child is entitled to be shown how to speak and write in standard English, yet the danger of devaluing home and community language must be acknowledged.

Spelling and handwriting

Children who are learning to read and write will obviously make spelling mistakes. Society as a whole is entirely unforgiving about spelling, and a business letter with a single error is produced as proof that the educational system is failing to teach literacy. So teachers have to ask themselves two questions, firstly 'How long do I tolerate error?' and secondly, 'What is the best way of teaching spelling?'

What do we do when we are unsure about how to spell a word? Usually our strategy is to jot it down and see if it 'looks right'. This is proof that spelling is a visual skill first and foremost, and those with a good visual memory will be the best natural spellers. Teachers encourage children to look at words and parts of words so that they can reproduce them in their writing. When children rely on the sounds of words they will spell in a phonic way which is quite understandable, but sometimes incorrect. An example might be 'I fort the dinosor wos very exsitin.' They may also write using mainly consonants, leaving out the vowels which are harder to distinguish. They may write 'I wnt to the bfrm to clen my tf.' Again, this is understandable, but the spelling will not improve if the children continue to rely on listening to the sounds of the words. Margaret Peters has written several books over a number of years in which she stresses the predictability of English spelling (Peters 1967 and 1985). Groups of letters, known as letter-strings, remain constant in words and can be isolated and learned. For example, 'here', 'there' and 'where' have all got 'here' in them. Endings like '-ible', '-able', '-tion', '-tious', cannot be heard clearly, but can be learnt as useful word-parts that are frequently met. Prefixes and suffixes can also be introduced to the children so they will be able to see that a long word is often no more difficult to spell than a short word: for example, 'unworkable', 'dislike', 'homeless'. Understanding the meaning of word-parts will also help spelling. Children who know that the prefix 'bi-' means two will remember that it is 'bicycle' and not 'bycicle'.

Most junior classes have some kind of regular spelling practice. To be most effective, the teacher must have a clear plan of campaign. You can think of the words in our language as falling into two groups: those that follow a spelling rule and those that don't. The first group can be taught in families, using the letter sounds (phonics) that have already been taught for reading, and adding the further rules gradually. There are many books which give a suggested order for these rules. The other group of words, the irregularly spelled words, have to be taught by the 'look-and-say' method. Many of these are the high-frequency words that make up the largest portion of any text. Think of the word 'done', for example. If it was regularly spelled it would rhyme with 'phone'. No wonder children habitually write 'dun'. And why is it 'goes' and not 'gose'?

As well as learning to look carefully at words, children should be encouraged to use their handwriting to help their spelling (Cripps 1988). There is evidence that children with a swift, neat style of writing are more accurate spellers. The momentum of the hand as it draws its way through the word helps to produce the correct letters. A joined style is obviously needed for the writing to flow. Some schools are starting to teach joined writing from the reception class. This avoids the problems children have when they move from unjoined script to joined writing. Whatever the system, handwriting needs to be taught regularly and carefully. The teacher really does need to watch the child as he or she is writing, and not just look at the finished piece of work. This is the only way to correct children who are writing letters the wrong way round. If they persist in bad habits like this they will find joining-up very difficult.

Reading skills

An experienced reader brings more to the text than he or she takes from it. This is to say we pick up so much literacy knowledge in our reading lives that we know what we are going to read before we read it (Meek 1988). On seeing a women's magazine we know the kind of articles we will find inside. We may flick over the pages, starting at the back of the magazine, watching for an interesting picture to catch our eye. This is very different from the reading behaviour we have learned to use when starting to read a book for information. In this case, we may use the contents page to find the most relevant chapter, or perhaps the book has an index. We can only use the index if we have enough knowledge of the subject to understand the categories of the index. Once we start to read we take it slowly, possibly making notes to remind us of the main points. This, again, is quite different from the way we would read a detective novel before going to sleep at night.

Because we can predict so accurately what kind of text we are going to find in the various books and magazines we meet, we engage the right kind of reading style without thinking. This sophistication takes us years of experience, but children can be helped to acquire some of the necessary repetoire of skills. Teachers encourage children to begin to use the skills of skimming (quickly reading through to grasp the subject) and scanning (looking quickly down a text for some key-words or phrases. They also have to teach children that this technique would be a bad one to use when reading poetry, which requires slow, reflective reading and rereading.

DARTS

Teaching skills like these reading techniques has acquired the jargon name of DARTS. The acronym stands for Directed Activities Related to Texts. Some of the activities such as reading a text and answering questions about the content of it might strike you as familiar. Surely this is the traditional 'comprehension' that we did so regularly and tediously at school? Certainly, it looks the same, but the purposes have changed a great deal. When children answer questions on texts nowadays, they are encouraged to work collaboratively. They are told that there is no one 'right answer', but that there are alternatives which have to be discussed. Some questions may be answered by quoting directly from the text, but it is much more likely that the teacher will have written questions to help the children deduce and infer answers. By learning to 'read between the lines' in this way, children are taught to be much more active and reflective in their reading (Moy and Raleigh 1988). DARTS are often devised using pieces of text about the topic subject. For example, a year 6 class might be asked to look at some descriptions of the seaside town they are going to visit for a study week. These descriptions come from a nineteenth century guidebook, a modern guidebook, an architecture book and a sailing manual. Differences of style and content will be noticed and debated, and the children will learn a lot about writing for different purposes and audiences. Another valuable source of texts for DARTS activities is fiction. By using carefully selected extracts from novels, children can begin to see how characters are described, how landscape can be evoked to create a mood and how small details can build into a larger picture that can be shared by a reader. These insights will make their subsequent reading and writing more deliberate, more informed, and more enjoyable.

Information Retrieval

The last aspect of language learning which needs to be explained is that of learning how to be an efficient researcher. Again, this work can be usefully linked to the topic subject that is being studied. Researchers, even if they are children, need to understand how to locate, select, organise and evaluate information. This means they will have to know how to use a book's index and contents pages, how to use the classification system in the library, and what to expect from encyclopedias, dictionaries, and reference books in general. The skill of note-taking is one that can be taught to children as young as eight. They enjoy taking a notebook with them to watch a video for example, and can begin to jot down a few points. Teachers who take time to explain these things will encourage independence and active learning in the children. Children also need to learn how to make the best use of computers, both as providers of information, and as processors of data which the children input.

Summary

This chapter has described the different aspects of language learning in junior classes. The emphasis is on learning how to engage with a wider variety of written material than was possible in the first stages of learning to read and write. Teachers of juniors have to have a professional and critical approach to the kinds of fiction and non-fiction that are available, and be able to devise ways of using suitable texts in order to teach a variety of reading skills. Children need to be shown that the purposes and intended audience of a text influence its style. They will then be able to use this awareness in their own writing. This chapter also considers the growing need to work towards standard spoken and written English.

CHAPTER 7

Science

The study of science in the primary school is a fascinating part of the curriculum, and it has great interest for the children. You may feel rather daunted by the prospect of teaching science, especially if you did not do much at school. However, it is now one of the three core subjects of the National Curriculum and must be studied from year 1. This chapter will introduce you to some of the ideas that underlie the National Curriculum for science. It speaks of 'matters, skills and processes'. This can be paraphrased into 'knowledge, skills and understanding'. Knowledge is of limited use on its own. You probably know that H_2O is the chemical name for water, but could you explain what this means? Skills are the tools that are needed to investigate scientifically. Understanding is necessary in order to think creatively about the subject being studied.

Contexts

Children are introduced to science by asking them to think about their everyday experiences. Children are naturally curious, and will have been investigating their environment from the first time they carried a rattle to their mouths. Familiar events and processes from their homes or from school are discussed. Visits are arranged to places of interest where the natural or the created world can be examined. Industrial processes are analysed, and in this way, many mysteries are unravelled. All these subjects are introduced to the children in a practical way. At every point there are opportunities for the children to experiment or observe for themselves. This is how they will develop the skills needed to be thoughtful scientists. It will be worthwhile to mention some of these skills now.

Skills

Using senses

Children have very sharp senses, but they do not always know how to use them scientifically. With guidance, they can begin to make sensible observations. Objects can be sorted and grouped according to their similarities and differences. This is just what children like to do when they collect sea shells or play with granny's button box, but at school the task may be more thought provoking. Some differences like the different hardness of rocks, or the different porosity ('waterproofness') of building materials, might not have occurred to them. Children can also be asked to use their senses when they are walking through a wood or along a path. Thirty pairs of eyes and ears can see and hear much more than one person alone.

Communication

Although the National Curriculum is arranged by subject, it cannot be taught by keeping each subject in its own little box. When children tackle a scientific piece of research, they are being asked primarily to think, and then to put their thoughts into words. This form of precise communication is not often demanded in other fields of study, and it needs a careful use of words which children may find difficult. When you hear them describing a 'thingummy', or a 'whatsit', and waving their arms around in an attempt to explain something, you realise that it may be necessary to give them some new vocabulary to cope with the situation. The learning of new terms and the ability to put logical thoughts into words are language skills, but they are very suitable for practising during science lessons.

Questioning

An important part of scientific method is the ability to ask questions and to answer them. Young children at home love to ask 'Why?' and this should be encouraged at school too. As other children search for a reasonable answer, they will be making hypotheses that may or may not be correct. The evidence may lead children to infer the wrong conclusion as to why something is happening. This is often because their scientific knowledge is not wide enough to allow them to make the right inference. For example, a child who knows nothing about magnetism might infer that the magnet is sticky. Being right or wrong is not nearly as important as looking at the evidence, and using reasoning and logic to suggest an answer.

Recording

There are many interesting ways to record scientific data. Infant children can add squares to a bar graph and build up a graphic display that shows clearly what has been discovered. As they get older, children will need to learn about other ways of showing data, such as frequency tables and pie charts. The teacher can encourage clear presentation of data by her own displays on the walls. Data can also be fed into a computer which can then print out tables and charts which are much more accurate than a child could draw. Colour printers make these diagrams even more appealing.

Research into children's writing has shown that they find it easier to write stories than accounts. The word that has been used for narrative writing is 'chronological' because it describes things that happen through time, and thus time is itself an organiser of the events that are being written down. Faced with writing 'non chronologically' children are said to find it difficult to know how to organise their ideas. Writing accounts of scientific experiments can be seen to be a valuable way of getting children to organise their thoughts. There will be chronology in the writing because obviously the setting up of the experiments comes at the beginning, and the results and comments on the results come at the end. This is narrative without the 'story' element that children are used to, and will help them learn the writing skills needed for future essays and possibly dissertations.

Practical skills

There are many opportunities when exploring scientific ideas to use practical skills. The handling of tools and materials has to be taught carefully. There is some truth in the old saying that a sharp knife is less dangerous than a blunt one because it does its job properly, but even so, the children have to be shown how to use the knife. Making models and apparatus to test a theory is very satisfying for many children, and is an ideal way of encouraging co-operative group work. The children also have to learn how to use the various tools of measurement when they come to take readings from their experiments.

Controlling variables

The idea of a 'fair test' is one that comes gradually to children. Many things will need testing in experiments: strength, hardness, flexibility, solubility, weight, volume, speed. If the children are asked to design a test they will have to get to grips with many of the problems that face all scientists. First, they will have to formulate a testable hypotheses. Then they will need to work out how to control other variables in order to make the test a fair one. For example, children may be testing materials for friction. They put blocks with different surfaces on a slope and see how steep the slope has to be before the block will slide down. But the blocks are not all the same size or the same weight. Do any of the children comment on this, and how will they test to see if it makes any difference? Teachers should themselves be aware of the various factors that can affect the results of an experiment. It is amazing how much discussion the simplest experiment can create, and how often an experiment can produce unexpected results because of unforeseen factors.

All the skills mentioned above will develop as the child grows older. Skills of investigation and measuring do not develop in isolation. They need to be taught within the context of a particular scientific topic. This makes the choice of activities very difficult for teachers, for so often an experiment will need more sophisticated measuring or understanding than the children possess at that time. For example, children might be asked 'Which paper towel soaks up most water?' Seven-year-olds could find out which one, but ten-year-olds could also find out the area of the paper towel and the volume of water soaked up. It is well worth looking for ideas in published science materials, particularly if you do not feel very creative in this field.

The National Curriculum for Science

Before we look at the National Curriculum in detail, we need to be clear about the vast area the subject covers. It is helpful to divide it up into themes. The National Curriculum suggests the following:

Materials and their characteristics
Living things
Forces and their effects
Earth science
Energy

Alternatively, the subject could be divided into larger themes:

The environment
Materials
Processes at work
Variety of life

Children need to be introduced to each of these areas, and to work regularly on aspects of them.

We can now begin to look in more detail at the specifications of the National Curriculum. Science has four Attainment Targets and each of these Targets has several strands of knowledge included in it. The first Target is the one that describes the skills necessary for scientific investigation. The other three Targets deal with what has traditionally been studied under the titles of biology, chemistry and physics. Taking Target 4, physical properties as an example, the strands of knowledge are:

i   Electricity and magnetism.
ii   Energy resources and energy transfer.
iii Forces and their effects.
iv   Light and sound.
v   The Earth's place in the universe.

If this sounds a daunting list, here are the suggested statements of attainment at the level 3 stage. Level 3 is the end of Key Stage 1 and is typically reached at the end of infant schooling (the end of year 2).

i   know that a complete circuit is needed for electrical devices to work.
ii   know that there is a range of fuels in the home.
iii understand that forces can affect the position, movement and shape

of an object.

iv   know that light and sound can be reflected.

v   know that the appearance of the moon and the altitude of the sun change in a regular and predictable manner.

These five statements do not sound too difficult for a typical seven-year-old to understand, and you can probably think of some interesting activities which would give the children useful experience of these physical processes. To show the effect of forces, for example, children could investigate toys that are powered by elastic, wind up and by electrical motors. They can see that these are manufactured forces, and compare them with the force of gravity and the force of their own muscles that power their bodies. The children will already have an instinctive knowledge of how things move from their early play, but now they can begin to question why and how, and to see similarities between things (an elbow joint and Tower Bridge for example).

The contribution of science to the curriculum

It is strange but true that no one would consider it necessary to write a chapter justifying the place of mathematics or English in the core curriculum. Science on the other hand, has gained its foreground place in the primary curriculum only recently, and many infant and junior teachers have had to do quite a bit of homework in order to prepare themselves for teaching. The Non-Statutory Guidance of the National Curriculum for Science (1989) lists the following contributions that science makes to the curriculum.

Understanding the key concepts

If pupils explore ideas in a range of contexts they will come to a cognitive understanding of key concepts. This will stand them in good stead for approaching unfamiliar situations.

Using scientific methods of investigation

These are the skills that are described in Attainment Target 1 (scientific investigation). They have already been described at the beginning of this chapter, but briefly they include: observing, questioning, measuring and devising a fair test. The same methods can be used in other subject areas, for instance design and technology.

Appreciating the contribution science makes to society

The history of the applications of science is a fascinating story of the cleverness and hard work that has gone into every step of 'progress'. Moral and ethical issues can also be explored by older children.

Learning in science contributes to personal development

Science education teaches nurturing attitudes such as willingness to tolerate uncertainty, co-operation with others and the critical appraisal of information. Scientific investigations are the best means by which to help children reflect upon evidence and learn to make hypotheses. The field of health education is an important part of science teaching in the primary school, where children learn about growing up.

Appreciating the powerful but provisional nature of scientific knowledge and explanation

Children will find excitement in scientific discovery and realise just how established explanations were found. They will also see that there is always a place for amending or modifying scientific models of the world.

Giving students access to careers in science, and design and technology

Early science learning may well motivate children to pursue the subject throughout school and on to university. Our advanced technological country needs all the scientists it can educate.

Equal opportunities

> Pupils and teachers not infrequently perceive boys as performing better at CDT (Craft, Design, Technology) than girls. One reason for this may be the greater confidence with which boys tackle design-and-make activities. If the teacher herself is lacking in experience of and confidence in the use of tools and materials, she may well mistake confidence in this area for competence.
> (Bridget Egan 1990).

Although this quotation is about technology, the same point could be made for science activities. In many cases, it is not the teacher's expectations of boys and girls that differ, but it is the girls' own low expectations of themselves which prevent them engaging fully in scientific work. At the same time the boys appear to know what they are doing, as Bridget Egan says, and the stage is set for extending the gender stereotypes into yet another generation. It is well established that the choice of learning context has a strong effect on pupils' performance. Teachers have to make sure that their presentation of scientific concepts is as 'girl friendly' as possible. Girls should be shown that they have all the requirements needed to be able scientists. For example, they can measure accurately and write coherent reports of experiments (indeed, they often out perform boys). They should receive praise for this, and encouragement to be more confident when making scientific suppositions. All girl groups are sometimes useful for experimental work. Strong images of female scientists should be available.

Range of teaching strategies

Encouraging communication

It has already been mentioned that the exploration of science is first and foremost a chance to improve communication skills. No amount of experimentation will be of any use unless the experimenter can share thoughts and findings with others, either in speech or in writing. Teachers need to acknowledge this before they set up the teaching situation. It is easy to overlook opportunities for practising communication when the class is busy with experiments. A good example of this might be a group working with batteries and bulbs to try and make circuits. All the children are avidly connecting wires to batteries, until sooner or later a bulb is lit. Other children watch and notice that there are two wires from the bulb, both going to different sides of the battery, and they copy this model to good effect. At this point have they understood the circuit principle? They have certainly made a start, but they now need to put their findings into words. They will need new vocabulary (circuit, current, terminal), and they will need to practice the explanation orally before they can begin to write it down. This holds true for children of any age, and adults too. So the teacher of the group working on circuits asks them to explain their findings to another group, or to her, and she makes sure they can use the new terms accurately before she concludes that the learning she hoped for has indeed taken place.

Experiments

Science teaching should not only encourage communication at every stage, it should also be as practical as possible. Children need to experience new phenomena or concepts in ways that use all their senses. They should be given the chance to touch and smell materials as well as look at them, although tasting should, of course, be avoided. Teachers have often taken this to mean that every child should get the chance to do every experiment. This is a good rule to work to, but it may not always be the way to make discovery exciting. For example, a class was finding out about dinosaurs, and wanted to know what fossils were and how they were made. The teacher took a small aquarium and a plastic dinosaur, and sprinkled different coloured layers of soil and chalk over the dinosaur. When he was covered completely, and aeons of time had supposedly passed and the soil had turned to rock, she simulated erosion by removing the layers of soil until the dinosaur was exposed again, and explained that the bones had been turned into stone. The children were fully engaged by this little drama. There was no need for them to bury their own dinosaur, for they were informed and motivated by the demonstration.

Books

The careful teacher will also consider the best way to use books in any scientific work. As with experimenting, it is easy to ignore chances for practising communication. All teachers resource their topics with books, but they do not always make the best use of them. Here are a few ideas to help children get the most from books:

1. Put bookmarks, with a brief comment written on them, in the books. ('The third paragraph explains about the atmosphere on several planets.')
2. Photocopy paragraphs from books and stick them on cards with similar explanations.
3. Ask children to compare the treatment of the same subject in various books. They may find that a book for very young children actually falsifies information in its attempt to simplify it.
4. Have a session on reviewing all the reference books on the subject you are studying. Ask the children to give marks out of ten for print size, vocabulary, use of pictures, style, whether there is an index. Ask them to note also the date of publication. This will give the children a knowledge of which books are useful, and they will come to recognise good series and publishers.
5. Use portions of text about the science subject to make language exercises. Details of these activities are in the chapter on reading and writing processes.
6. After children read a part of a book for information, make it routine that they will then tell a partner what has been found out. This oral retelling is a test of whether the information has really been understood of whether it needs to be read again.
7. Show by your behaviour that you rely on books for information, and do not carry every bit of information in your head. Tell the children which books you have found useful, and be critical of other books.
8. Do not let the children copy text books unless they can make out a good case for it (for example, a list of plant names or a recipe).

Drama

A final teaching strategy which is very useful for scientific topics is the use of simulation or role-play. Ideally, a simulation should involve the complete transformation of the classroom into another environment for half a day or longer. You and the children both act in role. This is often done with older children to lend drama to a debate. The children become a town council, for example, and have to debate the methods of rubbish disposal that the town will adopt. Various people voice their vested interests, and this makes the children realise the complexity of any decision like this. Younger children will need a more dramatic transformation. The classroom could become a 'weather laboratory' in which 'experts' measure and record rainfall, wind direction and sunshine hours, recording their findings on tape for a 'local radio' broadcast. Or, more ambitiously, the whole class could go back in time to visit a community where cholera was still endemic. The discovery that some diseases are water-borne was of tremendous importance, and depended on the prior invention of the microscope. This and many other stories of discovery could be played out by the children.

Summary

This chapter has shown the range of topics which come under the 'science' subject heading in the National Curriculum. It has offered reassurance that these topics give scope for many valuable cross-curricular skills to be taught and practised. The scientific knowledge that the curriculum expects children to learn is shown to be accessible in that it stems from everyday experiences. And some teaching strategies are suggested that will make the most of learning situations while studying science.

CHAPTER 8

Mathematics

In our culture, it is rather shameful to admit that one has trouble with reading and writing, but acceptable to say that one is hopeless at maths. The world of mathematics, which is every bit as exciting and creative as the world of literacy, is hardly explored by many people. Is maths really a hard subject, or are people put off by bad teaching in their early years? How will you generate excitement and enthusiasm for maths in your classroom?

Primary teachers often choose their profession because they love reading and the world of books. They long to teach children the mysteries of literacy so that they too can enter the magical world. But teachers should be aware that not all children will follow the same route. There will be some in every class who find mathematical ideas just as (or more) exciting. They may get more pleasure and gain more self-esteem by working with maths than they get from reading. When teaching reading and writing, teachers actively work to bridge the gap between symbolism (the written word) and concrete reality (objects and action). They use picture clues, phonic families and so on. It is accepted that children need to possess both the oral vocabulary and the conceptual understanding of that vocabulary before they can be expected to use it in reading and writing. The same is true of maths vocabulary. The teaching of mathematics must be as thorough and varied as the best language teaching.

The nature of mathematics

It is very important that maths teaching should be structured. Maths is sequential in its knowledge. Everything that is taught, therefore, needs to be supported by what has gone before. It often happens that children are given a maths concept to work on, and the teacher suddenly realises that they cannot understand what to do because they are uncertain about simpler concepts that should have been understood properly before. For example, supposing a group of children has been asked to measure the length and breadth of the school hall, and given a 20-metre tape-measure. When they report back their findings, the teacher notices that they cannot convert the measurement on the tape (950cms, for example) to metres (9.5m). She suddenly wonders if they know how many centimetres there are in a metre, and does some quick questioning. As she feared, they are not sure, and she has to take the children back over earlier work in order to give them the necessary skills for the present work.

Sometimes, for motivational reasons and not through carelessness, a teacher might deliberately set a task which the children cannot complete because of a gap in their knowledge. Because they now have a *reason* to acquire that knowledge, they will be better motivated to do so. However, such a scenario is still one of structured teaching since the teacher has intentionally engineered the 'failure' of the children.

Of course, there will always be a need to revise previous work: no one expects learners to remember everything they have been taught in the past. And there may be other reasons why revision is necessary. Gaps in the sequential knowledge of maths can arise because children were absent when the subject was taught. This is why it is so important to keep detailed records of children's work. It is also necessary to make special provision for absentees when they return to school.

The language of mathematics

Maths demands precision, and the correct use of mathematical language is essential to ensure this precision. To make matters more difficult, the language of maths is reduced to mathematical symbols when it is written down. In poor maths teaching, the process of acquiring the vocabulary, understanding it and learning the symbol for it is often short-circuited. Sometimes mathematical symbols are used too soon, before the child possesses the conceptual meaning of the symbol rather than merely an oral *translation* of it. For example, a child may know that '+' means 'add', 'plus' or 'put together with', but has he or she grasped what actually takes place in these operations? Teachers must always relate back from the sign to the idea as a check on understanding.

In maths, familiar words often have a specific mathematical meaning. If these are not properly used and explained, the children will become confused and will not develop as mathematical thinkers. For example, the word 'shape', as it is understood in ordinary conversation, has to be defined more specifically in maths. Do we mean a flat or two-dimensional shape, or a three-dimensional shape? If it is three-dimensional then mathematically it should be called a 'solid shape'. Similarly, there is often confusion with the words 'less' and 'fewer'. In maths, 'less' should be used for continuous substances ('there is less water in this beaker than in that one'), while 'fewer' should be used for a number of objects ('there are fewer conkers in my hand than in Jamie's'). In fact, this is merely good grammar rather than a special mathematical use, but in ordinary speech 'less' is typically employed for both these situations. 'Fewer' is hardly ever used, by children at any rate, so you hear them say, 'I've got less sweets than you.' Children have to learn the proper use of the word 'fewer' as they play with apparatus.

Sometimes the exact mathematical definition of a word will be a new concept for the teacher who has not thought very much about maths before. In these cases, the teacher has to rehearse the use of the word to make sure that it is going to be used accurately with the children. An example would be the proper use of the terms 'take away' and 'find the difference'. To 'take away', you remove a certain number of objects from a given set. This can be done with counters or cubes, and is quite easy to understand. To 'find the difference', you have two unequal sets, and match one set with the other until you find that there are some counters that will not match, and this is the 'difference'. Both these operations are worked out abstractly by doing a 'subtraction' sum, but only one of them is actually subtracting something.

Teachers who refer to all subtraction operations as 'take aways' are not giving the children an accurate vocabulary, and will cause confusion. Neither are they developing a full conceptual understanding. It is not the 'taking away' aspect of subtraction that is most commonly used in real life situations, but the 'find the difference' aspect. For example, money transactions that involve giving change are all about 'finding the difference'. The shop-worker uses the 'counting on' skill which is taught in many classrooms, and finds the difference between the price and the money offered by thinking, 'The loaf cost 87p and she gave me £1 so that's 88, 89, 90, 100', and handing over the 13p change.

A teacher who comprehends the true complexity of learning to use mathematical language accurately will find ways of establishing a broad understanding of terms in familiar concrete situations before specific mathematical applications are presented to the children. To take the example of difference again, the children need to focus on differences between two objects before they are ready to consider the difference in mathematical terms. Colour, size, shape, texture, are all attributes by which objects can be compared, and there are sets of plastic shapes and figures specially manufactured to help infant teachers consolidate this work.

Conventions

Because maths has a symbolic language that needs to be explored and understood, many conventions have been devised to make the meaning of the symbolism clearer. This is especially important with place value. Have you ever considered how clever it is that just ten symbols are used to represent any number from nought to infinity? This is achieved by grouping ten units together to make one '10', and ten tens together to make one '100', and so on. Infant classrooms usually have Multibase or Diennes apparatus that children can use. These are commercially-made systems of making models of numbers in a concrete form. The units are little cubes of either wood or plastic, and the '10' is a rod exactly the same size as ten one-unit cubes stuck together. The '100' is a flat square exactly the same size as ten of the '10' rods placed side by side, or, of course, one hundred of the little one-unit cubes. Children can practise converting ten one-unit cubes into a single '10' rod. In this way they can see and understand that '14' is fourteen one-unit cubes, but can also be converted into a '10' rod and a group of four one-unit cubes, which is why '14' is written as it is. Obviously this grouping has to be done again and again in a variety of ways and contexts, until the child has a clear picture of what the symbolic numbers on the page stand for. They are delighted when they realise that they have the power to write 'big numbers' just by using the same ten symbols they have already learned. But they should not be using numbers over ten until they have thoroughly explored the notion of grouping.

Much of the cognitive confusion that children (and adults) have about maths is caused by moving from the concrete to the abstract too soon. You may remember learning ways of 'doing sums' which ensured the right answer. You may have learned to 'borrow a ten', when subtracting, or to 'put the one on the doorstep' when multiplying, but did you know what you were doing? These shorthand tricks are useful only when the abstract operation is underpinned by a thorough understanding of the concrete process. If children work on 'decomposing' ten by using apparatus, they will understand what 'borrowing a ten' actually means within the conventions of our place value system. There is no quick way to move children on to the abstract stage because it is a matter of assimilating the concepts. Nothing can be assumed in mathematical knowledge. For example, before children are asked to look at the difference between two sets, have they fully explored the idea of equivalence? It seems obvious to us that one set of seven will match another set of seven, but it has to be proved by the child over and over again in many different ways. Seven cups can be matched with seven saucers in the home corner, seven books can be given out to seven children sitting round a table, and pencil-and-paper exercises can be devised to practise this matching concept. For some children this 'conservation of number' may take some time.

Children also lose the sense of creativity and enjoyment which mathematics can offer if they do not have a 'mental map' which gives them an insight into the linear nature of numbers. Most teachers in infant classes have a 'number line' somewhere around the room, but there are many ways in which children can actually experience the pattern and the symmetry of the line. Counting forwards and backwards in twos and fives, building a line with some of the number tracks that can be bought, chanting not only 'ten, twenty, thirty . . .' but 'seven, seventeen, twenty-seven, thirty-seven . . .' and also 'ninety-seven, one hundred and seven . . .', will help the cognitive picture develop in the minds of the children.

Real world applications

As the children get older, there is a disappointing tendency for maths teaching to move away from concrete real-life situations to abstract pencil-and-paper calculations. There is enjoyment in working out 'sums', and in setting them out neatly in an exercise book, and this will always be part of maths teaching. But the practical activities of weighing, measuring, constructing models, collecting data, using compasses and protractors, and predicting outcomes will all play their part in consolidating the understanding of maths. It is much easier for children to talk about mathematical ideas when they are embodied in a practical activity. So a child might report 'The yellow block weighs 250 grams and 4 of them weigh 1 kilogram which is the same as the red block.' Later on the same child will be able to calculate that 250g x 4 = 1kg and to have a true understanding of what this means.

It is important that teachers have a sure conviction that the children are gaining understanding from the practical activities. There is a great deal of pressure for all maths work to be recorded, so that there is evidence in a maths book to show parents that progress is being made. Sometimes teachers feel very torn between giving children what they need in the way of maths experiences, and following a more traditional path of exercises and sums. The answer is to do both since the one complements the other in the child's growth in understanding – as well as satisfying anxious parents.

In the first edition of the National Curriculum for Mathematics (1989), there was an Attainment Target called 'measures'. This was abandoned when the curriculum was simplified in 1991, and now the same concepts are to be found included in the five Attainment Targets of using and applying maths, number, algebra, shape and space, and handling data. The teaching of measures is vitally important because this is the way in which maths is most regularly used in the real world. Employers are quick to accuse schools of failing if they find that their new recruits are unable to record and calculate in appropriate measures. Teachers who hear children say things like 'My dad is six centimetres tall', or 'I'm going to put two kilograms of flour in this pastry', should realise that there is much work to be done. Oddly enough, the change to metric measurement, which is much easier to use for calculation, has not resulted in children being able to work with measurement more confidently. Part of the trouble appears to be the difficulty in remembering (or rather conceptualising) that there are 100 centimetres in one metre, but 1000 grams in a kilogram. There is also the added complication that miles and pints are still much more usual than kilometres and litres in everyday life.

Teachers can do much to help children by encouraging them to choose appropriate measures, and regularly asking for estimates of length, weight, distance, time and volume as part of the everyday discussion in the classroom. Because measuring is all about the real dimensions of the real world, the subject lends itself to display. The height of doors and the length of cupboards can be labelled clearly around the room. Photographs and wallcharts can be used to show other objects with their heights and weights and capacities displayed.

Children love to know the highest, smallest, heaviest and deepest, as can be seen by the popularity of the *Guiness Book of Records*. It is easy for teachers to use this enthusiasm to consolidate some basic concepts of measurement.

Individual goals

Because children develop at different rates, their mathematical needs are going to vary tremendously. It has been estimated that by year 6 (10- and 11-year-olds), some of the children will be working in maths at a typical 7-year-old level, and some at a 14-year-old level. It is hard for teachers to make provision for a seven-year attainment spread. One solution has been to give the children graded work cards, so they can each follow the course at their own pace. This sounds like a good idea until you see it in action. Since every child is doing something different, there is little chance of collaborative work, so the opportunities for discussing ideas together are lost. Another disadvantage of this work card system is that the teacher tends to fall back on giving cards out rather than teaching the topics the cards contain. The only real teaching that is done is when children find the card incomprehensible, and ask for help. So the children have already found difficulty and felt failure, and the teacher, instead of preparing the ground for new concepts, is merely a troubleshooter.

As we have seen, understanding maths depends on high quality teaching, so time must be found for this teaching, however difficult this might be. One way is to start a topic with the whole class. The teacher might, for example, want the children to become more agile in their mental calculations of numbers, so she introduces a cardboard model that she calls a 'function machine'. This has an input slot and an output slot, and a window to display the function that the machine obeys. When the function is 'x2', the input of '4' becomes an output of '8'. Cards are pushed through the input slot, and reappear (with some help from a human hand) from the output slot. All the children enjoy this, and can take turns in being the hand behind the machine. If the teacher has grouped the children by ability, she can give them functions to work on that match their level of maths development. Her targets may be to get the poorest group to be able to multiply by two and ten; the next group may be asked to understand that multiplying by two can be reversed by dividing by two, and to learn the use of the words 'doubling' and 'halving'; the next group may be asked to predict the pattern of outputs. After seeing that '1(x3+1)=4', and '2(x3+1)=7' they are asked what will happen to an input of '3' and of '4', and to complete a chart. All these activites are recommended in the National Curriculum under Attainment Target 3 (algebra), and are at levels 3 and 4. After the initial motivation of the 'function machine', the appropriate work can be given to the children on worksheets or cards, or on a blackboard. There will also be pages of suitable work in textbooks. The groups will be working at different levels, but they will all have the teacher's attention at some time, and feel that they are part of the class.

Although children may work in mixed ability or friendship groups for much of the curriculum, they are often grouped by ability for maths. Teachers realise that maths is the most linear of all the subjects, and that teaching needs to be targeted precisely to a conceptual level. An example might be helpful. Suppose that a year 3 class (seven and eight-year-olds) is spending a few sessions learning about fractions. The teacher has put the class into five maths groups, a large 'top' group of eight children, three groups of six and a group containing the four lowest attainers. First the teacher finds out what the children can do, and then determines what the next steps should be for each group. Her ideas for activities are shown below, where group 1 is the most able and group 5 the least able. You will see that there is a growing emphasis on the use of conventional symbols for fractions, but even the most able children are still given plenty of real-life experiences.

Work on fractions, year 3 (Five groups in the class.)

Activity	group
Colouring $\frac{1}{2}$ or $\frac{1}{4}$ of shape	5
Cutting shapes into $\frac{1}{2}$s and $\frac{1}{4}$s	5, 4
Understanding that a unit fraction is one of a set of equal parts	5, 4
Make unit shape from a fractional part, $\frac{1}{2}$ or $\frac{1}{4}$	5, 4
Make unit shape from a fractional part, $\frac{1}{2}$, $\frac{1}{4}$, $\frac{1}{5}$, $\frac{1}{6}$, $\frac{1}{10}$	3
Identify which shapes cut in two are not cut in $\frac{1}{2}$	4, 3
Record $\frac{1}{2}$, $\frac{1}{4}$, $\frac{1}{3}$ in notation	4, 3
Divide Plasticence block into two, three or four equal weight parts	4, 3
Divide clock face into $\frac{1}{2}$ and $\frac{1}{4}$	3, 2
Divide 30 minutes and 15 minutes into fractions of an hour	3, 2
Divide lengths of string/paper into $\frac{1}{2}$, $\frac{1}{4}$,	5, 4, 3

Divide lengths of string/paper into $\frac{1}{2}$, $\frac{1}{4}$, $\frac{1}{3}$, $\frac{1}{5}$, $\frac{1}{6}$, $\frac{1}{10}$	2, 1
Divide given weights of Plasticene into two, three or four equal parts	2, 1
Divide whole set into equal subsets (eight into four subsets)	4, 3, 2, 1
Relate this to division ($28 \div 4 = 7$ so $\frac{1}{4}$ of 28 is 7)	1
Dividing cm into fractions of m	2, 1
Dividing gms into fractions of kg	1
Expressing '1' in various forms ('family of 1' ($\frac{2}{2}$, $\frac{3}{3}$, $\frac{4}{4}$))	1, 2
Adding fractions to make '1' ($\frac{1}{4} + ? = 1$)	1
Recognising equivalence ('fraction families')	1

The National Curriculum

The National Curriculum for maths has five Attainment Targets. Each of these deals with an area of maths that should be taught, while each area has three or four strands within it, which indicate the concepts that are being developed by the suggested work. For example, Attainment Target 4 is shape and space, which we might know better as geometry. There are four strands within this target: shape, location, movement and measures. The first stages or levels concentrate on letting the children explore the world of shape and learn the vocabulary. They learn to recognise symmetry (the movement strand), and to sort shapes and describe their properties (the shape and location strands). The measuring strand does not begin until level 4, which is typically reached at the top of the junior school. At this point children are taught to measure perimeters, areas and volumes.

Each Attainment Target has several Statements of Attainment at each level. These are the landmarks or learning objectives by which the success of the teaching can be measured. They do not indicate how this piece of learning should be approached. This is done by the Programmes of Study which accompany the Statements of Attainment. So the Programme of Study for the Statement 'Find areas of plane shapes or volumes of simple solids' (Attainment Target 4, level 4) is 'Find areas by counting squares and volumes by counting cubes.' At the next level (level 5), the Programme of Study for the same Statement is 'Find areas of plane figures (excluding circles), using appropriate formulae. Find volumes of simple solids (excluding cylinders), using appropriate formulae.' We can see from this example that the children are being asked to move from the practical to the symbolic stage in working out areas and volumes, just as they did in understanding place value at an earlier age. The Programmes of Study are very useful to teachers who want some guidance in how to achieve the Statements of Attainment. They deal with the 'matters, skills and processes' of mathematics: in other words they explain the 'how' rather than merely the 'what' of the Statements of Attainment.

Maths topics

Because maths is so sequential, it is easy to plan work that is always taking the children forward into new ideas. Good teaching should make time for revising and practising what has already been learned. There is much to be said for giving children investigative tasks. These will pose problems that the children have the tools for solving if they can work out what they need to do. Working collaboratively, they can spend hours or even days on a well-thought-out investigation, and it will be very worthwhile both mathematically and socially. As the National Curriculum for Mathematics says: 'Different personal qualities are developed by tackling tasks of varying length and complexity. It is useful for pupils to experience the satisfaction both of instant success and the rewards gained from perseverance with the in-depth study of extended pieces of work.'

Using an investigative idea from a maths scheme or a book of ideas is fine, but sometimes it is fun to invent an investigation that is linked with other parts of the class's work. There is often scope for planning and measuring investigations based on the school buildings or grounds. Children are very inventive when asked to design ponds or play areas. After measuring the perimeter and area of some flowerbeds or some rectangles chalked on the playground, the question could be put, 'Do rectangles with the same perimeter always have the same area?' If you are unsure yourself, draw a rectangle 8cm long and 2cm wide, and another 7cm long and 3cm wide, and work out the area in each case.

Sometimes it is possible to devise some maths work based on a favourite book that you may be reading to the class, or that the children may be watching on video or listening to on cassette. Roald Dahl's book *The Witches* has inspired a class to make up potions for various magic cures. The teacher took the opportunity to get in some consolidation work on units of capacity. Each bottle had to contain a litre of potion, and the separate ingredients (coloured water with various magical names) had to be measured and recorded on the label. Local or national events (a new bypass, the Olympics) are also good motivation for maths work. In preparing this kind of work the teacher often has to decide what it would be appropriate to investigate, bearing in mind the age of the children. For example, the construction company building the bypass may give some statistics willingly, but it might be better to make up imaginary wage and work rates if the children are going to work out costs. Apart from the confidentiality of such data, it is usually necessary to give children simplied figures to work on. For younger children, simple ideas like cooking food for a teddy bears' picnic can be all the stimulus they need to enter into some useful weighing and measuring calculating ('If one bear eats three sandwiches and two cakes, how many . . .').

When planning a maths topic or investigation, it is important to be clear about the aims of the suggested work. The National Curriculum is written subject by subject, but there are many good reasons why you should plan work that encourages cross-curricular links. Perhaps you issue a challenge to make a container of a certain dimension from a given piece of cardboard. This will give children practice in making plans of solid shapes (known as 'nets' of shapes). But if the challenge is also to make the container strong enough to hold 500 grams when lifted by a handle, then this investigation has moved from the world of maths into the world of technology.

Calculators and computers

Calculators are part of the maths equipment in every school. This is not because children are incapable of 'working it out' for themselves, as some people think. The great usefulness of a calculator is its speed, so that patterns can be seen easily when, for example, the '+10' buttons are pressed several times. Up and down the number line, the calculator can reveal many insights into the world of number that a textbook would have to show in words and lists of figures. They can also be used for children to self-check their computations. Calculator work has to be carefully thought out, and there are many good books full of ideas.

Similarly, a computer is only useful if it has programmes that are applicable to the work going on in the class. It can consolidate concepts and provide great motivation to practise a specific skill. Colour and graphics are used so inventively in programmes nowadays that it is great fun to 'play' the games. Other programmes take data from the children (for example, their height and age) and will print out graphs and tables. Again, this is not providing an 'easy way out' for children, but is helping them to understand how individual statistics can be collected to build up a wider picture. Some schools have impressive colour printers which can be used for eye-catching design work.

Display and materials

Many maths investigations will appeal to the children much more if they are well-resourced and the display in the classroom reflects the work being done. Some teachers find display a chore, and are reluctant to change what is on the walls merely for a fortnight's topic. But for the children it is exciting to come to school to find the room transformed in some way. Some new backing paper and a bold topic title is all that needs to be done at the beginning of the topic; the children's work will soon be ready to fill the wall. Maybe they are going to make flow charts to show how they imagine a factory process works (how chocolate gets on to the top of biscuits; how holes are put into Maltesers; how the sticks are put into lollies). Maybe they are going to design a brochure to advertise an activity holiday (detailing prices for travel, accommodation and activities). Perhaps they are collecting tables and graphs from newspapers, and finding out what they represent. Perhaps they are drawing scale plans of the classroom or the school. Most maths investigations will involve producing some kind of display, and producing it to a good standard is an important part of the work. It helps children to feel that their efforts are valued by the teacher. Displays also provide a focus for class discussion, which in turn helps the children to consolidate key concepts and develop communication skills.

Using maths games is a wonderful way of keeping children's interest high while they perform what are really quite tedious repetitions of computation skills. Children never seem to tire of throwing a dice and moving a counter round a race track, or along a road to the buried treasure. It is quite easy to devise a few boards with these tracks around them, with places marked where children have to pick up cards. The cards can be changed to suit the subject the children are practising so that the board can be used again and again, and not only for maths games of course. Another simple way of engaging the children's interest is to get them to generate their own numbers to add or multiply by throwing a dice. A child that might slowly and reluctantly do five calculations from a page in a textbook or a worksheet will do twenty similar sums with this dice method.

A tremendous amount of high quality colour printing is thrown away in our society. Teachers must be the only people who consider how they can reuse some of the brochures and magazines that surround us. Promotional leaflets from garages are excellent for pictures of cars and lorries to illustrate a transport theme. Shops will often give away out-of-date placards and tickets to make a shop topic authentic. Bus and train stations provide holiday pictures as well as timetables. Tourist offices and information centres will be very generous with leaflets and maps. Children love to write away for literature, and they usually get a good response if they write from the school address.

Motivating children to enjoy maths and feel successful is often a journey of discovery for the teacher as well. Maths is creative, and comes from thinking about practical activities and from the world outside the classroom. It only comes from textbooks when a new process or skill needs practising. It has its own language and its own conventions which are satisfying to use accurately. It can be represented graphically in all sorts of ways (graphs, pie charts, matrices, bar charts) and these charts can be displayed and discussed. Some activities apply maths to a problem, while others are purely mathematical. Maths is embedded in daily life as deeply as language, and children have a need to be numerate, just as they need to be literate, in order to enter fully into adult life.

Summary

This chapter has loked at the importance of numeracy and stressed that maths is a 'doing' subject, and should not be made too abstract too soon in the children's school life. The difficulties some new teachers find are discussed and the special problems of mathematical language are explored. The huge variation in levels of maths attainment is mentioned, and it is suggested that children are grouped according to their ability. Some suggestions for activities are made, and the place of maths investigations, and other topic ideas are discussed, along with the importance of display and games.

CHAPTER 9

Developing Topic Work

Almost every school in the country uses a 'topic' approach in some form or another. What does this mean? If there was one definition of a 'topic' then the answer would be simple. But the term is used for many curriculum organisations and teaching styles. You may remember from your own primary school-days that you worked on 'centres of interest', or 'themes', or perhaps 'integrated work'. All these names have been given to what is now called topic work. What is the exact definition of a topic?

Topics can last a week, a month or a term. They can be worked on by individual children, groups, a class or a group of classes, or by the whole school at once. The topic work can occupy the whole available teaching time or it can be limited to an hour once or twice a week. Under the umbrella name of 'topic work' every imaginable school activity can take place, from essay writing to camping, from embroidery to staging a three-act opera.

How topic work developed

Forty years ago, before 'child-centred education' had been thought of, primary schools, unaffected by the constraints of GCE exams as secondary schools were, had the responsibility of deciding and planning what was taught. For maths and English, skills, concepts and knowledge had to be taught in some kind of order. Schools either produced their own syllabus for these subjects, or relied on using some of the many textbook series that publishers produced. This left the other subjects to be taught in some way. In many schools they were hardly taught at all, because the teaching of the 'three Rs' was seen as the main function of the primary school. A minimum amount of time, perhaps one session a week, might be spent on art, craft, games and P.E., and there would have been some history and geography taught in a fairly random way.

Gradually teachers saw that there were two ways on which the quality of education could be improved. The first was the move to child-centred methods of teaching, in which the interests and thus the motivation of the child was seen as a vital ingredient. Secondly, teachers began to identify and to map out the knowledge, skills and concepts that formed the foundation of such subjects as geography and history. By choosing a focus that would interest children, teachers found that they could provide a good grounding in all the subjects that the children would be studying more formally in the secondary schools. The idea of topic work had been born, and it continued to flourish throughout the seventies and eighties. Classrooms were turned into castles, submarines, rabbit holes, and children dressed up as Saxons, Vikings, Tudors, space-people, dragons, and any number of other characters. The 'success' of these imaginative flights of fancy would be hard to measure. Children certainly enjoyed themselves but what were they learning? The best teachers never lost sight of the learning objectives that underlay the topic, and they built in to the fun an amount of factual knowledge and practice for various skills. Other less clear-sighted teachers got carried away with the dressing up and the acting. At the end of a month spent making a model motte and bailey castle, and enacting the Battle of Hastings on the school field, children would still be unclear about whether William was a Norman or a Saxon. Did this matter?

It certainly did, and schools that were negligent in providing a rigorous learning framework for their topics, or which allowed children to 'do dinosaurs' twice in different classes were doing the reputation of state education no good at all. Children have a right of access to a broad and thorough curriculum. Topic work, if it is to be used, must be planned with the general aims of the National Curriculum in mind. These are continuity, progression, relevance, differentiation and coherence. At the same time topics must have a collection of overt teaching aims or objectives that cover the skills, knowledge and processes of the various subjects. The general opinion among the teaching profession is that the National Curriculum has identified and demanded coverage of far too many attainment areas, but nevertheless, the legislation is in place, and has to be followed. Teachers meeting together after school to plan future topics now have copies of the relevant National Curriculum subjects firmly open beside them.

Topic balance

In order to address all the subjects effectively, it is usual to plan for topics which have different subjects at their core. For example, a class may have a geographical topic to study for half a term, followed by a short scientific topic for three weeks and then move to a historical subject for the rest of the term. The geographical topic (perhaps it is 'Our Estate'), may provide lots of opportunities for measuring, and drawing plans and maps, but not much in writing continuous prose. The scientific topic which follows (maybe 'Birds in Winter'), is not only an opportunity to look at habitats and food chains, but also to respond emotionally to the amazing facts about the migratory journeys of winter visiting birds. Children might well draw and write poetry with this kind of stimulus, but the teacher might be aware that they are still not writing at length.

The last topic of the term, (let's say it is 'Edwardian England'), is taught through narrative, and the children watch videos of an Edwardian family and learn about class differences, housing, transport and a little of the impact on families of the First World War. This topic is designed to let the children write accounts and stories, and the teacher encourages this aspect. The emphasis of this topic could just as easily be science, giving children an introduction to machines that help with housework, for example, or early experiments in flight. But in this case, the teachers planning the year's work have decided to make this not only the place where certain historical concepts are taught but also the time when narrative writing is encouraged. It is rather like our consumption of healthy food: we need a balanced diet, but we do not need to eat greens at every meal.

Topics and the National Curriculum

The beginning of the nineties, with the implementation of the National Curriculum, has been a time of clarifying learning objectives in topic work. From its inception, the National Curriculum for Primary Schools was envisaged as a collection of subjects, each with its own syllabus as in secondary schools. This seemed to assume that primary schools would give up their topic-based approach and revert to a style of subject teaching that had long been dead. But many schools had already worked out a programme of topics that provided the kind of 'balanced diet' mentioned in the previous paragraph. School curriculum development teams had also spent hours of time after school devising and resourcing a broad selection of topic areas, so that no child need ever say 'We did that last year.'

When the curriculum was more flexible there was a trend towards giving children wider topics to work on. Often a whole term would be spent looking at 'change' in as many aspects as possible. Or perhaps an Infant school might work for several weeks on 'ourselves'. These wider and less-focussed topics were very valuable, because they suggested connections between concepts that might not be noticed in subject-based work. For example, a favourite all-embracing topic used to be 'holes and cavities'. Children studied animals' holes, birds that nest in holes, drain covers and sewers, honeycombs, hollow-stemmed plants, caves, and even invented imaginary machines to put the holes in Maltesers or macaroni. Nowadays there is little time for such broad-based topics, but there is still a place for the imaginative teacher to make topic activities as exciting as possible. Indeed, this inspiration is the teacher's best weapon against the move back to subject teaching which the National Curriculum was designed to promote. Another favourite stimulus for topic work has also been squeezed out by the National Curriculum. This is the topic based on a story or a genre of literature. When children begin to explore the world of books, there is nothing more exciting than devoting a week or two to respond to a book through art, role-play, models, talking and writing. Children can go on imaginary journeys down Alice's rabbit hole, to Lilliput with Gulliver, under the floorboards with the Borrowers, or along the river bank with Mole and Ratty. There are so many good books for children today that the classics can get forgotten. Imaginative activities can give children a flavour of the secret worlds within these wonderful books, and this will not only encourage them to read the books for themselves, but ensure that the books stay alive for another generation.

Characteristics of topic work

Research

From what has already been said in this chapter, it may look as if topic work is just another name for any classroom activities which are linked by a theme. Surely there must be more to topic work than this?

Yes, the whole point of topic work is to provide active learning opportunities for children. It might almost be said that there is a fourth 'R' to be added to the familiar three, that of Research. The skills of research are the ones that make children into autonomous learners, so that when they leave school, even with the least promising conditions, they can ask the right questions and know where to look for the answers. Young children, even those who cannot read on their own, can be shown how to begin to research. A familiar example might be the jar of frogspawn that appears in most country classrooms is the spring. The teacher can say 'What questions do we need to ask about this frogspawn?' and 'Where will we find the answers?' In this way children will come to understand the basic needs of all living things (What does it eat? Where does it live? How does it grow? How does it reproduce?) and this will give them a pattern of questioning that will remain useful for all further studies. Where the answers are found (in natural history books, in encyclopaedias but not in such detail, by asking other people who are more expert), will also give the children valuable help in becoming independent learners later on.

Teaching research skills has to be done methodically. It is quite unfair to provide children with a box of books on flight, for example, and ask them to find out about propeller and jet driven aeroplanes without any prior help. Research materials need to be carefully selected, and the children will need specific teaching on what have become known as 'study skills'. Understanding a library's classification system, using an index, looking for the main idea of a passage, making a precis, and even understanding the conventions of captions to pictures (above, below, overleaf), all have to be explained and practised. A parallel strand of skills has to be taught in the field of information technology, so that children can make constructive use of computer databases and other programmes.

Setting up a piece of valid topic research is a lengthy business. Books have to be found that are easy enough for the children to read. This means that many excellently illustrated adult 'coffee table' books are useless unless you write a parallel text in simpler language which can accompany the pictures. Even books written for children often over-estimate reading ability and may need bookmarks to guide children to key passages. Small portable objects are very inspiring: children like to draw from observations, and learn a lot in the process. Museums often have a loan service that can provide real or replica historical artefacts for a few weeks. This kind of evidence from the past is known as primary source material. It provides not only an accurate picture of what things were like, but it carries with it a sense of the past coming to life in the researcher's hands, which is very exciting for children. First-hand documents, even if they are just photocopies, are also powerfully evocative. Photographic evidence is obviously invaluable for giving an accurate picture of the past. Letting children use a camera on walks and outings is a good way of bringing a personal record of an experience back into the classroom. The fuzziest and crookedest images are studied carefully when the photographer is a school mate. Videos are an excellent source of information, but they are often too long. Rerecording a few minutes of a BBC wildlife programme could provide study material which the children could watch several times to emphasise main points of the subject.

If a teacher spends hours finding resources like these that are appropriate for the age of the children, it makes sense to keep the work and make it available for other classes. Knowledge, skills and processes of all the subjects that are taught in the topic can be identified. This is how many schools have answered the demands of the National Curriculum without sacrificing the valuable multi-subject approach which is the hallmark of good primary teaching in this country.

Collaborative work

Topic work is, almost by definition, work which is undertaken collaboratively. This is the way to ensure that the children use every opportunity to debate and discuss alternative strategies and outcomes. Although it is rewarding to end a topic with wonderful models, paintings and written work about the room, in terms of learning it is the quality of the processes by which these things were created that is significant, not just the products themselves. The children should also be involved as much as possible in resourcing the topic. Bringing things from home is part of giving the children a feeling of ownership about their work in school. Families, too, like to feel that their experiences are being valued by the school, and will lend the most treasured heirlooms very trustingly, which can be something of a worry for the teacher. Involving the community in any study of local history or geography will often pay enormous dividends as residents offer their reminiscences and local knowledge.

Organising a class for group work needs careful thought. It has been noted already that often, when a teacher thinks children are working as a group, they are merely working individually around the same table. The task they are working on should ideally be of an investigative nature which will encourage hypothesis and suggestion around the group. Yet even when the task is suitably exploratory, there are many ways in which the group may sabotage the teacher's well-intentioned plans. Researchers have noticed how common it is that a few assertive children monopolise the discussion, leaving others silent and unengaged. Again, it has been seen that boys are prone to take the lead in certain subject areas. How can a teacher positively discriminate in favour of girls when the class is working on a technology project? Is there a place for single-sex groups in such cases? And is it best to have groups of the same ability or to ensure that there is a mix of abilities? There are no 'answers' to these questions, but the aware teacher will bear them all in mind when deciding how to organise the work.

Having planned a series of activities for a topic, it is natural that the teacher should want every child in the class to do every activity. On reflection this might not be the best way of working. Children love to be 'experts', and it can be arranged for different groups to become expert in different facets of the topic subject. So, for example, one group might conduct a survey of birds on the school field, and present their findings to the class after ten days or so. Another group could look at a video about migration and do some further research on their own. A third group could find the answers to questions which the whole class poses, like 'How long does an egg take to hatch? or 'Do birds get wet in the rain?' A fourth group could plan, and maybe make, a bird-table or a nesting-box. When all these investigations have been shared with the whole class, there is no need for each group to then do the other group's work because the children learn from each other, as well as feeling proud of their own achievement. There may well be other activities in the topic which every child will work on, such as drawing from observation, or completing a chart about the habitat and diet of various birds. All in all, the topic should provide a balance of activities across as many areas of the curriculum, and practising as many skills, as possible. The most important thing to remember is that, educationally, it is the process that matters and not the products.

Cross-curricular skills

The National Curriculum mentions skills that should be practised in many subject areas. Some of these skills have already been discussed in this chapter, but they still need identifying clearly. Here is a list in no particular order of importance:

1. Study skills
2. Information retrieval
3. Communication
4. Problem-solving
5. Observation
6. Personal and social skills
7. Numeracy skills
8. Literacy
9. Oracy

It could be argued that topic work is the ideal way to ensure that these skills are taught and practised. It could be argued more strongly that without topic work, some of these skills would be in danger of being ignored. If, as has been suggested, the National Curriculum is rewritten to specifically call for subject teaching in the areas of science, technology, history and geography, for example, then there will be no place for topic work in the primary curriculum. It is up to teachers, if they believe in the topic approach, to show that they are prepared to be accountable for both subject knowledge, concepts and skills, and cross-curricular skills in their topic teaching.

The teacher as enabler

The characteristic that most distinguishes topic work from other class work is that it actively involves the children. The teacher sets up learning situations, and then makes herself available as an 'enabler'. In this role she is an adviser and critic, allowing the children to suggest methods and solutions, and to make mistakes. She has already provided the best environment for learning that her resources will allow. Now it is up to the children to explore their powers as investigative learners.

This is a rather idealised picture, and it is doubtful if this style of working would be all that was needed to produce a successful topic.

There will be times when the most 'enabling' thing a teacher can do is give the class a lesson on the subject under consideration. If we take the subject of 'bridges' as an example, we can see how the teacher could plan some work. The room could be provided with plenty of construction sets and good quality materials for box-modelling. She could set some investigations in motion with a challenge to build a bridge capable of carrying a given weight across a given span. There would also be books and pictures available, showing the children the variety of constructions which have been devised to make bridges strong enough. At some point, however, the topic would be broadened by giving some direct teaching. Maybe the teacher could introduce a narrative thread into the information, and tell an edited version of the life of Isambard Kingdom Brunel, or perhaps Thomas Telford. Some of the successes and failures of innovative bridge designs in the nineteenth century make wonderful stories. Bridge building will be seen as a real historical activity, not just a classroom task involving string and straws. In this way children are not only asked to work with the full range of their own resources, but they are led to new knowledge and understanding. Topic work, when thoughtfully prepared and taught, is a method which is both effective and appropriate for primary children.

Summary

In this chapter the characteristics of topic work have been explored. Some of the changes brought about by the National Curriculum have been mentioned. The need for planning is stressed, both in the area of resources, and in order to cover subject knowledge and cross-curricular skills. There are also some suggestions about the possibilities of collaboration with families and the local community.

CHAPTER 10

Left on the Shelf? School Policy Documents and the National Curriculum

Teaching is a very personal skill. Every teacher likes to choose the activities and the methods that suit her style best. Every classroom has its own atmosphere. No amount of standardisation by means of a National Curriculum will change this, because teaching is an art and not a science. Teachers will only give of their best if they have the freedom to use their personalities as part of their teaching skills.

It was because primary teachers were able to please themselves about what they taught and when, that the government felt the need for a National Curriculum for all state schools. In following their own interests, often with great dedication and skill, teachers were not always providing a breadth of learning. There were too many instances (some undoubtably fictitious), of children 'doing the dinosaurs' twice or even three times in their primary school life. Of course, well-organised schools have always avoided this repetition by planning ahead as a whole school.

Since the National Curriculum has been implemented, schools have had to rewrite their policy documents. The progression of skills in literacy and numeracy should now match with what the National Curriculum expects children to achieve at the various levels. But it is not just concepts and skills that are mandatory. The subjects covered by topic work will have to coincide with those specified in the National Curriculum. If it states that children in year 3 should study tadpoles and frogs, then the teacher will not be able to pursue her favourite topic of butterflies and moths, or at least, not in much depth and not taking up much time.

Although teachers have been critical of the way the National Curriculum was implemented in the late 1980s and early nineties, they acknowledge that, in its amended form, the Curriculum makes sense. It is obviously better if children can move school and find the same work being done. It is also useful for teachers to have guidance on what to include in each subject's syllabus. Teachers will be studying the National Curriculum and the school policy documents as they plan their term or half term's work. The Programmes of Study in the Curriculum suggest how specific activities could be carried out to ensure a broad range of learning opportunities.

Teachers may now feel constrained, but they have to admit that there are dangers in being too personal when doing the job. Because you know what 'feels right', it is easy to be dismissive about other methods, materials and schemes of work. You feel that a ready-made worksheet will never be as good as the ones you devise yourself, which are specifically aimed at the needs of your class. A published maths scheme or history pack never seem to be quite what you want. So you spend hours in the evenings making worksheets. And on Saturdays you go to museums and art galleries in search of pictures and information. This dedication is admirable, but it may not always be entirely necessary. Ask the families of teachers. You may well find resentment at the amount of time they spend in preparing their school work. The title of this chapter is chosen to alert teachers to ways of saving themselves unnecessary work, and also to make the best use of the resources they collect.

Subject co-ordinators

Every school has teachers who are paid an allowance to be specialists in the different subject areas. In a small school, the same person will be responsible for several areas of the curriculum, and they may well argue that they should be paid more than one allowance but this does not happen. Part of the job of these subject co-ordinators is to devise a policy document for their subject, which everyone in the school uses as the basis for their teaching. The English guidelines, for example, will explain the school policy on reading, spelling, handwriting and the use of the library. It is essential that every teacher in the school uses these documents when planning their work. This is the only way that a school can make its philosophy of learning work in a coherent way. If the teachers ignore the guidelines, and teach in a purely personal way, then the school is nothing more than a collection of classes. Head teachers should make sure that newcomers to the staff plan their work

98

following the guidelines of the school.

Resources

When you next go into a school, see if you can look around the staffroom and stock-room shelves. There may be topic boxes, video and sound recordings, posters and other published resources. Schools often spend a lot of money buying materials that are underused. Even if the materials do not look as if they are exactly right for the children, they can be adapted. Often history and geography packs have excellent pictures but the text is too hard for children to read independently. With a word processor it is very quick to write simpler text to go with the pictures. It is well worth checking the available resources to save valuable time.

Some of the resources you find in schools will be home-made. Now that the National Curriculum has defined the range of subjects, this in turn defines the topics that a school will choose to study. This is a golden opportunity to collect useful worksheets, textbooks and artefacts into 'topic boxes' that can be used over several years. Teachers are very good at preparing materials for their own class, but not so good at sharing them. Subject co-ordinators should try to foster a 'whole school' approach to collecting resources. If the home-made materials are valued by the school then teachers will take extra care in making them. For instance, anything made from card will have a much longer life if it is laminated with plastic. Big schools and teachers' centres often have a laminating machine. Any cards or posters with writing on should ideally be made using the schools's preferred writing style.

Record keeping

The first thing to emphasise is that records are only worth keeping if they are going to be used. The most important use for them is to help teachers find out what stage individual children have reached, and what they need to do next. This is yet another instance of the need to use all available resources, and not leave things on the shelf.

All teachers keep records for their own use as part of their planning, and in order to assess progress they often devise informal tests. The whole process could be thought of as circular: plan – teach – test – record – plan again. Schools often have a system of record-keeping that has been worked out by the staff over the years. It may consist of a series of statements to be ticked when a child can achieve them. Since the National Curriculum has been introduced, the Statements of Attainment are often used. These 'can do' statements are better than nothing if you want to plan work. But they do not tell you about the characteristic learning pattern of particular children. Did they manage the 'can do' statement easily, or after lots of practice? Did they ask for help from the teacher or from friends? Did they enjoy it? To build up a complete picture of individual children it will be necessary to write a few sentences in the record, and this takes much longer than ticking boxes. It is a good idea to keep a note book, with a page for each child. By jotting down a few phrases when something strikes you about the child's learning, you will find you have plenty of evidence of what the child can do and, more importantly, how he or she does it. You might write things like: 'Wrote two sentences on his own but still not punctuating', 'Counted in 5s up to 30 using apparatus', 'Used dictionary to find "garage"', 'Read story to class with expression.'

Assessment

The assessing of children is a very thorny subject. The reasons for assessing will obviously influence the way in which the tests are viewed. Many assessments are useful and benign. A teacher may well analyse a child's spelling errors in a piece of text, or even set a dictation exercise herself. The knowledge she obtains from this test will provide her with the means to plan the next phase of spelling instruction and practice. The child's spelling is not being judged against an outside standard and there is no intention to 'pass' or 'fail' the child.

However, other forms of testing are also used in schools. Here, the test is given in order to compare a child's attainment with a proven norm for the child's age. The test may be given to a whole class, or to the whole country's seven-year-olds, as in the National Curriculum Standard Assessment Tasks. The results can be shown in a table that lists all the children in rank order. Surely this would be interesting and just as valid as the spelling test described earlier?

The problem with 'norm referenced' tests like the Standard

Assessment Tasks (SATs) is that no allowance is given for the circumstances of the test, the ability of the child or the teaching that has taken place before the test. Indeed, the league table of test results may do nothing more than show which areas are advantaged and which disadvantaged. A simple 'attainment' score contains no indication of whether this is commendable for the child or not. In the first three years of running English SATs for seven-year-olds (Key Stage 1), the children who speak English as a second language had consistently lower scores. This is not surprising as they speak another language at home and may only begin to learn English (both spoken and written) when they come to nursery or infant school. Any school with a high proportion of second language learners will have poorer SATs results, regardless of its teaching, than other schools with only English speaking children. This will given an unfair picture of the success of the school, but more importantly, it will give an unfair picture of the progress of the children. It is as if we were to be given a test in French which marked us in the same way as French mother-tongue candidates.

Does this mean that all norm-referenced testing is inherently flawed and is not worth doing? Not at all. Country-wide testing can be a valuable way of indicating areas of teaching that need improvement. It may also show an upward or a downward trend in literacy or numeracy, and will indicate how British children compare with children educated under different countries' systems. Equally usefully, it may highlight methods of teaching in certain schools that are particularly successful and which would be worth adopting more widely. However, norm-referenced testing can never tell the whole story of children's achievement. This is why teachers, governors and parents have opposed the government's belief that testing on a national basis is the key to raising standards of teaching.

It is very common for students to begin their teaching practice by drawing up a grid listing the names of the children one way and the activities they intend to teach on the other axis. After using this tick sheet for a day or two, students realise that it isn't recording enough information to be useful. They decide to use a booklet instead, and begin to jot down information about the children as they notice them throughout the day. At this point they have moved from simple record-keeping to more useful assessment. Nothing is formalised, but by making sure that each child goes 'under the microscope' regularly, students can build up a written picture of the child's learning pattern. From these notes they will be able to write an accurate report at any

time it is needed. Teachers who have been involved in the Key Stage 1
testing, repeatedly say that the tests tell them nothing they did not
already know about the children's strengths and weaknesses.

Summary

This chapter explains that planning in schools is best done
collaboratively, and resources shared. Students are encouraged to make
use of any helpful documents they can find in school, including the
National Curriculum. The links between record-keeing and assessment
are discussed, and the form and purpose of various kinds of assessment
are mentioned.

References

Alexander et al (1992) *Curriculum Organisation and Classroom Practice in Primary Schools: a discussion paper* (London: HMSO).

Bealing, D. (1972) 'Organisation of Junior Classrooms', *Educational Research,* **114**, 231-235.

Bruner, J. S. (1966) *Towards a Theory of Instruction* (Cambridge, Mass. and London: Balknap Press of Harvard University).

Bryant, P. and Bradley, L. (1985) *Children's Reading Problems, Psychology and Education* (London: Blackwell).

Bullock (1975) *A Language for Life: a Report of the Committee of Inquiry appointed by the Secretary of State for Education and Science under the chairmanship of Sir Allan Bullock* (London: HMSO).

Clay, M. (1972) *Sand and Stones: Concepts about Print Test* (Auckland, New Zealand: Heinemann).

Clay, M. (1979) *The Early Detection of Reading Difficulties* (New Zealand: Heinemann).

Cripps, C. (1988) *A Hand for Spelling,* Bks 1-4 (Wisbech Learning Development Aids).

Edwards, D. and Mercer, N. (1989) 'Reconstructing Context: the conventionalisation of classroom knowledge', *Discourse Processes,* **12**, 91-104.

Egan, B. (1990) 'Design and Technology in the Classroom: Equalising Opportunities' in *Dolls and Dungarees: Gender issues in the Primary School Curriculum,* ed. Eva Tutchell (Milton Keynes: Open University Press).

Galton, M. (1987) 'An Oracle Chronicle: A Decade of Classroom Research', *Teaching and Teacher Education,* **3** (4), 299-313.

Goodman, Y., Watson, D., Burke, C. (1987) *Reading Miscue Inventory, Alternative Procedures* (New York: Richard C. Owen).

Graves, D. (1983) *Writing: Teachers and Children at work* (London: Heinemann Educational).

HMI (1982) *Bullock Revisited: a Discussion Paper* (London: HMSO).

HMI (1990) *The Teaching and Learning of Reading in Primary Schools* (London: HMSO).

Hornsby, B. (1988) *Overcoming Dyslexia* (London: Optima).

Iser, W. (1978) *The Act of Reading: a Theory of Aesthetic Response*

(London: Routledge and Kegan Paul).

Kerry, T (1981) 'Talking: the Teacher's Role' in *Communicating in the Classroom*, ed. Sutton. C. (London: Hodder and Stoughton).

Kouin, J. (1970) *Discipline and Group Management in Classrooms* (New York: Holt, Reinhart and Winston).

Mackay, D., Thompson, B., Schaub, P. (1978) *Breakthrough Teachers' Manual: the Theory and Practice of Teaching Initial Reading and Writing* (London: Longmans for the School Council).

Meek, M. (1982) *Learning to Read* (London: Bodley Head).

Meek, M. (1988) *How Texts Teach what Readers Learn* (Stroud: Thimble Press).

Moon, C. (1992) *Individualised reading: comparative lists of selected books for young readers* (23rd edition) (Reading: Reading and Language Information Centre).

Moon, C. and Raban, B. (1992) *A Question of Reading* (London: David Fulton).

Moy, B. and Raleigh, M. (1988) 'Comprehension: Bringing it Back Alive' in *Language and Literacy from an educational perspective* (Vol 2, *In Schools*), ed. Neil Mercer (Milton Keynes: Open University Press).

Ofsted (1993) *Curriculum Organisation and Classroom Practice in Primary Schools: a follow up report* (London: HMSO).

Peters, M. (1967) *Spelling Caught or Taught?* (London: Routledge and Kegan Paul).

Peters, M. (1985) *Spelling Caught or Taught? A new look* (London: Routledge and Kegan Paul).

Plowden, Baroness B. (1967) *Children and their Primary Schools: a report of the Central Advisory Council for Education, England,* Vol. 1 (London: HMSO).

Pumphrey, P., Peter, D. (1992) *Specific Learning Disorders (Dyslexia): challenges and responses, a national enquiry* (London: NFER Routledge).

Rogoff, B. and Gardner, W. P. (1984) 'Guidance in Cognitive development: an examination of mother and child instruction', in *Everyday Cognition: its Development in Social Context,* ed. Rogoff, B. (Cambridge, Mass.: Harvard University Press).

Rosen, M. (1989) *Did I Hear you Write?* (London: Andre Deutsch).

Simon, B. (1981) 'Why no Pedagogy in England?' in *Education in the Eighties: the Central Issues,* Simon, B. and Taylor, W. (London: Batsford).

104

Smith, F. (1982) *Writing and the Writer* (London: Heinemann Educational).

Tizard, B. and Hughes, M. (1984) *Young Children Learning: Talking and Thinking at Home and School* (London: Fontana).

Vygotsky, L. S. (trans. 1962) *Thought and Language* (Cambridge, Mass.: M.I.T. Press).

Waterland, L. (1985) *Read With Me, an Apprenticeship approach to Reading* (Stroud: Thimble Press).

Wells, G. (1986) *The Meaning Makers: Children Learning Language and Using Language* (London: Hodder and Stoughton Educational).

Wilkinson, A. (1965) 'Spoken English', *Educational Review Occasional Publications, 2* (University of Birmingham School of Education).

Index